CW00689173

THE INFINITE'S ASH
CENIZA DE INFINITO

Para Charlie,
con el agradecimiento
y el cariño de
Víctor Rodríguez =
Brimingham, 11 de
octubre de 2011

Víctor Rodríguez Núñez

THE
INFINITE'S
ASH

CENIZA DE INFINITO

&

Translated and introduced by
Katherine M. Hedeen

Arc
PUBLICATIONS
2008

Published by Arc Publications,
Nanholme Mill, Shaw Wood Road
Todmorden OL14 6DA, UK

Design by Tony Ward
Printed in Great Britain by the MPG Books Group,
Bodmin and King's Lynn

978 1904614 62 3 (pbk)
978 1906570 06 4 (hbk)

ACKNOWLEDGEMENTS

Grateful acknowledgement is made to the editors of the following journals where the previously uncollected poems first appeared: 'Metaphysics', 'To the Memory Of' and 'Snapshot' in *The Bitter Oleander*; 'Self-Portraits', 'Conjectures on a Pastor's Smile', 'Umbrellas', 'Guilt Complex', 'Legend', 'Slogans' and 'Trade Secret' in *Mid-American Review*; 'Marco Polo's Dilemma' in *The Kenyon Review*; 'Entrance', 'Hypothesis', 'Poem for Emily' and 'Tarot' in *Denver Quarterly*; 'At Times', 'Epilogue' and 'Nights' in *New York Quarterly*; 'Countersign' and 'Certainties' in *Chelsea*; 'Naval Engineering' and 'Cantina in Cochabamba or 'Llorando se fue' in *The Cream City Review*; 'Eulogy for the Neutrino' in *The Literary Review*; 'Prologue' and 'Logic' in *The New England Review*.

The publishers acknowledge financial assistance from
ACE Yorkshire

Arc Publications Translations Series
Translations Editor: Jean Boase-Beier

To our children,
Eduardo Lázaro,
Luis Alfonso
and Miah Anjélica

CONTENTS

from / de
THE LAST TO THE FAIR
EL ÚLTIMO A LA FERIA

from / de
CEASELESS PRAYER
ORACIÓN INCONCLUSA

INTRODUCTION

In the text that opens this selection of the early poetry of Víctor Rodríguez Núñez, one of today's most relevant Cuban writers, the subject recalls an event that he could not have witnessed: the appearance of Halley's Comet in 1910. In this significant 'Prologue', material phenomena and their spiritual registry are first represented by the grandmother's orality, and later on, by the writing of notable Spanish poet Rafael Alberti. At the vertex of these two visions of the world, symbolizing the past and present, the objective and subjective, the lived and imagined, the private and public, the popular and cultured, is this author's work. We are before a poetic will to overcome certain traditional contradictions, to negate determined negations of dominant ideology and aesthetic.

Víctor Rodríguez Núñez was born in Havana in 1955, but did not grow up there. When he was a year old, he and his parents moved to Casilda, a small sea port in the southern-central part of Cuba. And a few years later, as a consequence of his parents' separation, he went with his mother to live at his maternal grandparents' home in Central FNTA, in the same region. The poet recognizes a neighbourhood of that tiny town, built up like many in Cuba around a sugar mill, as his true country: Cayama. There his life was marked by the values of a community of immigrants (Galicians, Japanese, Portuguese) and their Cuban descendants, half way between working class and farmers. Above all he learned, as he recognizes today, "to be a part, but not to belong, to be a bit removed from everything, to not see things only from the inside, to return to a place I never left."[1]

When he was eleven, Rodríguez Núñez was pulled away from that world, making even more profound his sense of vagabondage, separation and foreignness, which still persists. He finished his education at different boarding schools on the island and graduated in sociology from the Universidad de La Habana in 1979. His first job was as a philosophy professor at the Universidad Central de Las Villas, but he left it almost immediately to become a journalist. During the 1980s he was writer and editor of *El Caimán*

---

[1] Interview with Víctor Rodríguez Núñez, 17 December 2007.

Barbudo (The Bearded Caiman), the most influential Cuban cultural magazine of its time, where he published dozens of articles on literature and film. There he confronted Stalinism and the dogma of Socialist Realism which, as a consequence of the Cuban revolutionary government's alliance with European socialism, distorted the essentially decolonizing character of the transformative process initiated in 1959.

Rodríguez Núñez's first book of poems, *Cayama* (Santiago de Cuba: Uvero, 1979), was part of a trend in the renewal of Cuban poetry which has still not been sufficiently studied: the so-called 'tojocismo'.[2] A poetry written from the countryside and the peasant condition, it confronts urban verse and the interests of a middle class prevalent in Cuba since the end of the nineteenth century. It is a book written under the fundamental influence of Spanish poetry from the first half of the twentieth century, particularly by Antonio Machado, Federico García Lorca and the above-mentioned Alberti. In this collection abound eminently lyrical and monologic short poems, with a depurated language filled with the speech of the Cuban countryside, representing the reality of the neighbourhood where the author grew up. Cayama would later become a mythical space and time, present throughout his work.

Nonetheless, the book that places Rodríguez Núñez's verse within Cuban poetry is *Con raro olor a mundo* (With a Strange Scent of World) (Havana: Unión, 1982). In 1980 it received the recognition that any young Cuban poet would want: the David Prize. Its texts display a displacement from 'tojocismo' to the so-called 'conversational' poetry, which has been evolving in Spanish America since the 1950s. This unites participative content and formal experimentation, approaches popular culture and recognizes the reader as co-author of the work. Its language makes use of orality, as well as the lexicon of the social sciences and mass media, and rejects Pablo Neruda's epic monologue to affirm César Vallejo's dialogic lyricism. With his third book, *Noticiario del solo* (Lonely

---

[2] In Cuban Spanish, 'tojosa' means mourning dove, a common bird of the island's countryside, and often present in this poetry.

Man's News) (Havana: Letras Cubanas, 1987), which includes the poems that, in 1983, won the then coveted prize of the Mexican journal *Plural*, he moved even closer to the conversational poetry of the Cuban Fayad Jamís, the Argentine Juan Gelman and the Salvadorean Roque Dalton.

Rodríguez Núñez has always been interested in the work of other poets. In the pages of *El Caimán Barbudo*, he extensively published the verses of his contemporaries and, above all, selected, edited and wrote the prologues to three notable anthologies.[3] In reference to this endeavour, Walfrido Dorta points out that to be familiar with Cuban poetry from the 1980s it is impossible to overlook "an anthology like *Usted es la culpable* (You are the Guilty One)", especially if this kind of book is considered a way "to make a group, a generation or a poetic visible". We cannot forget that *Cuba, en su lugar la poesía* (Cuba, Poetry in Its Place) had previously appeared, "which in a certain way had already announced other discursive possibilities".[4] Even so, the most extensive and profound of the three is *El pasado del cielo* (Heaven's Past), crafted with a more heterodox and inclusive critical perspective, and which unfortunately has not circulated in Cuba.[5]

Rodríguez Núñez has also written numerous essays on Cuban poetry from the 1980s and 1990s that can be read not only as a critical assessment but also as an exposition of his own poetic.

---

[3] *Cuba, en su lugar la poesía: Antología diferente* (Cuba, Poetry in Its Place: A Different Anthology) (Mexico: U Metropolitana-Azcapotzalco, 1982), *Usted es la culpable: Nueva poesía cubana* (You are the Guilty One: New Cuban Poetry) (Havana: Abril, 1985), and *El pasado del cielo: La nueva y novísima poesía cubana* (Heaven's Past: The New and Newest Cuban Poetry) (Medellín: Alejandría Editores, 1994).

[4] 'Almas y centros: poesía y crítica.' (Souls and Centers: Poetry and Criticism) *Cuba Literaria*. 23 December 2007. www.cubaliteraria.com/es/ elacubaficha.php?s_Autor= Walfrido+Dorta&Id= 1478

[5] The most relevant poets of Rodríguez Núñez's generation are Raúl Hernández Novás, Luis Lorente, José Pérez Olivares, Soleida Ríos, Reina María Rodríguez, Efraín Rodríguez Santana, Abilio Estévez, Alex Fleites, Marilyn Bobes, Ángel Escobar, Roberto Méndez Martínez, Ramón Fernández Larrea, Sigfredo Ariel, Alberto Rodríguez Tosca, among others.

The latter consists of principles that essentially have not changed, but rather have only suffered readjustments and variations, and that continue to guide his tireless writing. He still searches for, in his own words, "a poetry that is autonomous yet not unaware, participatory yet not political, subjective yet not intimist, structured yet not hermetic, communicative yet not explicit, lyrical yet not ahistorical, dialogic yet not conversational, Cuban yet not essentially nationalist, open to the world yet not colonized."[6] This is the work of a poet who dissents from the European version of socialism, and also from exploitation and repression, from plundering imperialist wars, art for art's sake and from all assaults on freedom and beauty.

From 1988 to 1995 Rodríguez Núñez lived in Nicaragua and Colombia, where he edited the journals *Wani* and *Revista Universidad Cooperativa de Colombia* and established strong ties with these countries' intellectual communities. Such experiences ultimately determined the opening of a new poetic cycle – what he has called his "mester de extranjería" – which is made up of *Los poemas de nadie y otros poemas* (Nobody's Poems and Other Poems) (Medellín: Tecnológico de Antioquia, 1994), *El último a la feria* (The Last to the Fair) (EDUCA Prize, Costa Rica; San José: EDUCA, 1995), and *Oración inconclusa* (Ceaseless Prayer) (Renacimiento Prize, Spain; Seville: Renacmiento, 2000). For Carlos Espinosa Domínguez, these collections mark "a point of inflection in his work. By that time, the author had left behind his adolescent phase and the lyric I of these poems summoned the acute perception of a divided, torn man."[7] Moreover, returning to the author's own words, there is the certainty that "nations are a mirage and that nationalism is ultimately oppressive." [8]

---

[6] Rodríguez Núñez, Víctor. 'Teque número tres.' (Spiel Number Three) *Renacimiento* 51-54 (2006): 134-36.
[7] 'Con olor a buena poesía.' (With the Scent of Good Poetry) *Encuentro en la red* (Encounter Online). 14 May 2007. 23 December 2007. www.cubaencuentro.com/es/encuentro-en-la-red/cultura/articulos/con-olor-a-buena-poesia.
[8] Interview with Víctor Rodríguez Núñez, 17 December 2007.

Rodríguez Núñez's poetry has been well-received in the Spanish-speaking world. For the Colombian poet Juan Manuel Roca, "[t]he core of this poetry is its lyricism, the way in which it ennobles the most daily acts and moves them to the plane of poetic creativity. It is a war of the world in language and language in the world, a battle against death and oblivion."[9] The Argentine poet Jorge Boccanera considers that "Rodríguez Nuñez's poetry has a singular expression. Here, the quotidian becomes intimate, celebrated and profound. While the common is expressed with a familiar language, this poetry never loses its intensity; it is sustained by images of great force and beauty."[10] And for the Cuban poet José Pérez Olivares: "One cannot analyze Rodriguez Nuñez's poetry in the same way as the work of other poets from his generation... It refutes the purely literary and aesthetic realm and enters into that of human conduct. It is this and not cultural referents which nourishes his poetry."[11]

Rodríguez Núñez has resided in the United States since 1995, not as a political exile but as one of the thousands of the world's intellectuals linked to the country's academic institutions. In 2001 he received his doctorate in Hispanic Literatures from The University of Texas at Austin, and has taught that specialism at Kenyon College ever since. At the time of writing, he has opened a third cycle that, as he himself recognizes, constitutes "a radical change in my poetic, a very different poetry than the one I had been recognized for in the past."[12] It is made up of the two volumes of the extensive poem *Actas de medianoche: Actas de medianoche / I* (Midnight Minutes) (Valladolid: Junta de Castilla y León, 2006),

[9] 'Postal de medianoche' (Midnight Postcard). *Los poemas de nadie y otros poemas* by Rodríguez Núñez. Medellín: Tecnológico de Antioquia, 1994. 3-7.
[10] 'Backpage.' *Los poemas de nadie seguido de El último a la feria* (Nobody's Poems followed by The Last to the Fair). By Rodríguez Núñez. Havana: Letras Cubanas, 1999.
[11] 'El tigre que acecha al ciervo inalcanzable.' (The Tiger that Lies in Wait for the Unreachable Deer) *La Gaceta de Cuba* 2 (2001): 59.
[12] Interview with Víctor Rodríguez Núñez. 17 December 2007.

and *Actas de medianoche / II* (Soria: Diputación Provincial de Soria, 2007). Both have been awarded prizes in Spain, the Accésit of the Fray Luis de Leon Prize and the Leonor Prize, respectively.

With regard to *Actas de medianoche*, Rodríguez Núñez has said: "Up until that point my work had consisted of short poems that I always visualized as a structure, that revolved around a concept, and that followed a strict organization. Here I let my consciousness flow, unrestrained, except for a rhythm, which is mine, based on verses of seven, eleven and fourteen metric syllables."[13] The main theme of the first part of the poem is "differentiation", which the poetic 'I' considers to be the first step in the process of constructing an identity. The second half deals with "identification", without which no identity is complete. Rodríguez Núñez continues: "the poem is a conversation with the night, which embodies all kinds of otherness. Its form is based on the Spanish sonnet, and for that reason there are fourteen cantos, one for each verse of the sonnet, and each canto is made up of eleven free-verse sonnets." Espinosa Domínguez has noted that "we are before a work of singular ambition, experimental method, and extension." [14]

Rodríguez Núñez is also an essayist, literary critic, and translator. His essay on Gabriel García Márquez's non-fiction, *Cien años de solidaridad* (One Hundred Years of Solidarity), was awarded the

<hr/>

[13] 'Entrevista a Víctor Rodríguez Núñez.' (Interview with Victor Rodríguez Núñez) *Revista de Soria* 56 (Spring 2007): 93-95.

[14] In this regard, Espinosa Domínguez adds: "In his earlier books, Rodríguez Núñez had achieved a writing that despite being sustained by suggestive images of great force, always conserved the capacity to communicate with the reader. It is a clear, warm poetry without renouncing mystery, capable of clean expression and with a softly conversational language without losing intensity or lyrical strength. In *Actas de medianoche*, however, the author opts for a discourse that is difficult to access, which changes it to a discourse confined to itself. Rodríguez Núñez has stated that necessities of expression are what led him to assume the risks of an experimental work like *Actas de medianoche*." In conclusion, he writes: "We are by no means before a failed work or a false step in the trajectory of a poet of an unquestionable maturity. On the contrary, the fact that he has taken the risk to try out other roads should be saluted as a demonstration of clear growth."

Enrique José Varona Prize in Havana, in 1986. He has published various critical editions, introductions and articles on Spanish American poets. His research focuses on how modern and contemporary poetry from the region has represented and subverted different kinds of social subordination, using as a theoretical and methodological basis for this textual analysis a broad range of postcolonial, gender, ethnic and gay perspectives. Among his translations are Margaret Randall's *Esto sucede cuando el corazón de una mujer se rompe* (This Happens When a Woman's Heart Breaks) (Madrid: Hiperión, 1999); and John Kinsella's *El silo: Una sinfonía pastoral* (The Silo: A Pastoral Symphony) (Havana: Arte y Literatura, 2005) and *América o el resplandor* (America or Glow) (Havana: Torre de Letras, 2006), with Katherine Hedeen, both of which were first published in the UK by Arc Publications.

The present translation is based on Rodríguez Núñez's selected poems, *Con raro olor a mundo: Primera antología, 1978-1998* (With A Strange Scent of World: First Anthology, 1978-1998) (Havana: Unión, 2004), which offers a representative sample as well as a rewriting of his early poetic work. I agree with Espinosa Domínguez that "throughout these texts their author is able to maintain a voice, a style, and a rigour." In that collection the poet excluded texts from *Cayama*, and for this reason they are not considered here, the first of his books to appear in English. Likewise, as this is a sample of his early poetry, I have chosen to not include texts from *Actas de medianoche*. In the present work, I have been fortunate to count on the valuable collaboration of the author. I hope to have not betrayed him, to have been faithful to the meaning of his poems and at the same to have made them sound as if they were originally written in English. These are poems that are at once committed and experimental, where every limit is challenged, and where emotion and lucidity, what is another's and one's own, Neruda and Vallejo, the author and the reader, come together.

Katherine M. Hedeen

THE INFINITE'S ASH
CENIZA DE INFINITO

I

from / *de*
WITH A STRANGE SCENT OF WORLD
CON RARO OLOR A MUNDO

PRÓLOGO
a *La arboleda perdida* de Rafael Alberti

Cuando el cometa Halley
ese viejo maleante de los cielos
cruzó a navajazos el vientre de la noche
mi abuela
        que aún no era la abuela
de nadie en este mundo
soñó tener su limpia cabellera
y puso en el mortero seis huevos de gorrión
que volvió
        quién sabe cómo
            polvo enamorado
para rehacer su rostro húmedo
a la triste manera de la luna

Pero en otro rincón de este planeta
que gira como un enjambre de avispas
cuando el cometa Halley
guardaba ensangrentada de noche su navaja
un niño gaditano con ojos de bahía
quiso peinar la rauda cabellera del cielo
con su tridente de marinero en tierra firme

Ha tenido que pasar
        desesperado
           el siglo
han cicatrizado las heridas de la noche
el niño no es el niño
        sino un viejo
poeta del destierro que regresa
la abuela no es la abuela
sino una abeja
        que aguijonea el alma
a otro niño que peina en el recuerdo
la limpia cabellera
        de una noche del mundo

PROLOGUE

for Rafael Alberti's *La arboleda perdida*

When Halley's comet
old bandit of the skies
cut night's belly with his switchblade
my grandmother
     who still was not the grandmother
of anyone in this world
dreamt of clean hair
and put six sparrow's eggs in her mortar
that became
   who knows how
     love dust
to reshape her humid face
like the sad way of the moon

But in another corner of this planet
spinning like a swarm of wasps
when Halley's comet
put away his switchblade
     bloodied with night
a boy from Cadiz with bay-like eyes
wanted to comb the sky's swift hair
with his trident of a mariner on land

The century has had to pass
     desperately
night's wounds have scarred
the boy is not the boy
    but an old man
a banished poet who returns
the grandmother is not the grandmother
but a wasp
   stinging the soul
of another boy
    who combs in memory
the clean hair
    of one night in the world

21

¿DÓNDE?

¿A dónde habrán ido mis juguetes
los de la cuerda rota por la lluvia?
¿Vivirán
       en el fondo del mar como naufragios
en el fondo del cielo
            cual luceros de vidrio
en el fondo del río como cangrejos verdes
en el fondo del fuego
          cual ceniza de espanto?
¿O en el fondo de mí
       como fantasmas?

WHERE?

Where have my playthings gone
those with the string rotted by rain?
Do they dwell
           in the sea's depths as sunken ships
in the sky's depths
           as crystal stars
in the river's depths like green crabs
in fire's depths
           as fear's ashes?
Or in the depths of me
           as phantoms?

DISTANCIAS

Qué lejos la ciudad
            el faro y las estrellas
el balcón en que ahora despeinará la noche
Y qué cerca los campos
el épico aguacero que termina
de derramarse gris sobre los árboles
y ese perro que ladra a la distancia

Qué lejos los amigos
la espuma mineral de la cerveza
– las noticias un nudo
para las manecillas del reloj
Qué cerca la familia
la harina de maíz
            el quinqué y las arañas

Qué lejos la mujer
          la que inventamos
más allá de la herida
Qué cerca la de siempre
cotidiana y feliz
deshaciendo el amor en cualquier sitio
con olor a naranjas

Qué lejos el poema
          – el espectro
la imposibilidad turbios cristales
Y qué cerca el vacío
          la madera
esa novela extraña
la impaciencia invisible de los grillos

Y qué lejos qué cerca
          la muerte de la vida

DISTANCES

How far the city
                lighthouse and stars
a balcony where now night tousles
And how close the fields
epic rains that have finished
spilling grey over trees
and a dog barking to the distance

How far friends
beer's mineral foam –
the news a tangle
                for watch hands
How close ancestors
corn flour
        oil lamp and spiders

How far the woman
                we invent
beyond the wound
How close the same one as always
quotidian and happy
unmaking love anywhere
with a scent of oranges

How far the poem –
                spectre
impossibilities turbid glass
And how close the void
                wood
that strange novel
unseen impatience of crickets

And how far how close
                death from life

TRENES

para María Isabel Borrero

> *y así corría el tren inmóvil*
> Pablo Neruda

Desde que amanecí
por casualidad a la muerte
                          fieros
y sólo para mí
todos los trenes silban

Los de niño eran convoyes de azúcar
terrones de madera al hilo en el portal
chirriando por la vía
                          que dejan las babosas
lentamente borrachas
rodando hacia lo puro
como palomas negras
                          sobre un cielo marcado
por relámpagos dulces
que comen las hormigas

En un tren me alejé de la colina
donde hoy no está mi casa
– ni perro color sucio que me ladre
ni abuelo carpintero
menos abuela con su aguja difícil –
sólo mamá despierta
algún olor a plátanos
                          cenizas y cebollas
mi hermano distraído
y cuatro tablas viejas de inviernos y cansancios
rosas artificiales
                          un radio con mi nombre
y el potrico del diablo que lucha con la araña

Incluso
          en el 70
fui retranquero loco

TRAINS

for María Isabel Borrero

> *and so the immobile train rolled by*
> Pablo Neruda

Since I dawned
            by chance
                        on death
fiercely
            and only for me
all the trains whistle

Those from my childhood were convoys of sugar
cubes of wood lined up on the porch
screeching along the tracks
left behind by slugs
                        slowly drunk
rolling toward pureness
as black doves
                        above a sky marked
by the sweet lightening bolts
                                    devoured by ants

In a train I left the hill
where my house is not today
– no dirty-coloured dog barking at me
no carpenter grandfather
no grandmother with her difficult needle –
only mama awake
a smell like plantains
                        ashes and onions
my distracted brother
and a few boards aged from winter and weariness
artificial roses
            a radio with my name
and a dragonfly fighting with a spider

Even
      in 1970
I was a crazy brakeman

conductor de mentira
con farol encendido por la lluvia
de trenes sonámbulos que violaban la sombra
deseable de toda madrugada
Me fui cuando cayeron estrellas en mis ojos
cuando las paralelas se cortaron
allá
   en el infinito
              – desnudo de rocío
de polvos adquiridos en velorios y puentes

Luego monté vagones
que me llevaron
          siempre
              de los huesos al sol
de enero hasta diciembre en primavera
de la ola a la nube que anida en la colina
de la luz a la piedra
           del agua hasta el silencio
de una destartalada
         fea
           y sucia estación
a la nombrada
        Estación Esperanza

Hace poco que un tren
me alejó del amor
– y debí
     no obstante
          agradecerle la bahía
cuajada por las luces
de los barcos que duermen
y que despertarán sin pesadillas
Y más tarde una palma
sobre la tierra roja que el tractor ha sentido
una casa redonda con laguna
            las cañas que florecen
y la cerca de púas que cuelga de una garza

                              a bogus conductor
with a lantern lit by the rain
of sleepwalking trains raping
desirable early morning shadows
I quit when stars fell in my eyes
when the parallel lines were cut
there
            in the infinite –
                              naked in dew
in dusts acquired at funerals and bridges

Later I rode train cars
that took me
                  always
                              from bones to sun
from January to December in Spring
from waves to that cloud nesting on the hill
from light to stone
                              from water to silence
from a rickety
                  ugly
                        dirty station
to the one named
                  Hope

Not long ago a train
distanced me from love –
and I should
                  nonetheless
                              thank it for the bay
thickened by the lights
of sleeping boats
that will awaken without nightmares
And later on for a palm tree
over the red earth touched by a tractor
a round house with a lagoon
                              the flowering sugarcane
and the barbed-wire fence hanging from a heron

Ahora este tren
                    nada vertiginoso
me acerca a la ciudad
de mis bodas de espuma
Del coche restaurante
                    tomo cerveza negra
huevos de chocolate
corazones dorados
                    que crujen en los dientes
mi pan de soledad
En la ciudad me espera una mujer
y en la mujer
                    un hijo

Algún día saldrá el último tren
Un convoy transparente
sin ruedas materiales
                    sin humo ni sonido
Seguro estoy
                Seré el único pasajero
Me sentaré en mi sitio
                    violento silbaré
Así devolveré lo que me han dado
estos trenes malditos

Desde que anocheció
por necesidad a la vida
                    tiernos
y sólo para él
todos los trenes silban

.

Now this train
            slow and steady
brings me ever closer to the city
of my sea foam wedding
In the restaurant car
                  I have dark beer
chocolate eggs
golden hearts
            the crunch in my teeth
my bread of solitude
In the city a woman waits for me
and in the woman
                  a child

Someday the last train will leave
A transparent convoy
with ghostly wheels
                  no smoke or sound
I am sure
        to be the only passenger
I will sit in my seat
                  violently whistle
so to return what they have given me
these wretched trains

Since I set
            by necessity
                        on life
tenderly
        and only for me
all the trains whistle

UN POEMA CON TIGRE

para Alex Fleites

Me persigue el tigre de Blake
el oro de su piel
                el fragor de su impaciencia

Ayer
      mientras llovía
asaltó una reunión de mi comité de base
y no quedó un papel en su sitio
– lo siento por las actas
                    yo las hago
Se bebió los ojos de un amigo
y de un zarpazo dejó desnuda a Esther
– precisamente a Esther –
y sus pechos de madera bendita
temblaron en el aire
con olor a naranjas que presienten el fuego

Me persigue el tigre de Blake
su poderosa respiración de astro
el ardor de sus garras

No terminaré nunca este poema

A POEM WITH TIGER

for Alex Fleites

Blake's tiger chases me
the gold of his skin
                    the clamour of his impatience

Yesterday
            while it rained
he attacked my committee meeting
and not one paper stayed in its place –
I feel sorry for the minutes
                        I write them
He drank the eyes of a friend
and with one blow of his paw left Esther naked
– precisely Esther –
and her breasts of holy wood
trembled in the air
with a smell of oranges foreboding fire

Blake's tiger chases me
his powerful breath of stars
the heat of his claws

I will never finish this poem

LÓGICA

Si he pensado
          cuando faltan las nubes
y cae algo así como polen solar
que un poema puede ser una muchacha
ha sido
      en esencia
porque ese mismo poema también
puede ser una fábrica
Sobre todas las cosas
si la fábrica es una muchacha
sonando sus sirenas
            contra el mundo
tendida a toda máquina sobre la hierba
– vapor ternura sueños –
quemando los aceites más dulces
                más difíciles
Para fundir una vez más la vida
y así
    lógicamente demostrar
cuando las nubes se cargan de polen
madurado de luz
que un poema puede ser
          ante todo
            un poema

LOGIC

If I've thought
               when clouds go missing
and something like solar pollen falls
that a poem can be a girl
it has been
          in essence
because that same poem
might be a factory
Moreover
          if the factory is a girl
sounding her sirens
               against the world
lying at full speed on the grass
– vapour tenderness dreams –
burning the sweetest
              most difficult oils
To once more melt life
and so
         logically demonstrate
when clouds are bursting with pollen
ripened by light
that a poem can be
           above all
              a poem

METAFÍSICA

Que me perdonen
                la hoja sin ventana
ese gato encendido en la azotea
el grillo equivocado
                la cal de las paredes
la sombra atormentada del último cometa
y mi profesor de filosofía
nervioso y lloviznado

Pero más allá de uno de tus besos
de aquellas pajaritas
que salieron volando de tus ojos
de tu pelo cortísimo
del árido bregar de las reuniones
de la almendra oscura de tus senos
más allá
              no existe la realidad objetiva

Sólo tú y el verde escalofrío de la nada

METAPHYSICS

May the shutter with no window
the cat in heat on the rooftop
the mistaken cricket
                    the lye on the walls
the tormented shadow of the last comet
and my philosophy professor
nervous and drizzled
                    forgive me

But beyond one of your kisses
those tiny birds
                    that flew from your eyes
your hair so short
the arid struggle of meetings
the dark almond of your breasts
beyond that
there is no objective reality

Only you
            and the green shiver of nothingness

HIPÓTESIS

Pensaba Ptolomeo
que el mundo era como el ojo de ciertas mujeres
Una esfera de húmedos cristales
en que cada astro describe una órbita perfecta
sin pasiones
                    mareas o catástrofes

Luego vino Copérnico
sabio que cambió senos por palomas
cosenos por espantos
y la pupila del sol fue el centro del universo
mientras Giordano Bruno crepitaba
para felicidad de curas y maridos

Entonces Galileo
estudiando a fondo el corazón de las muchachas
naufragó en el buen vino
– *luz aglutinada por el sol* –
violó estrellas que no eran de cine
y antes de morir sobre la cola de un cometa
sentenció que el amor era infinito

Kant por su parte no supo nada de mujeres
preso en la mariposa de los cálculos
en polen metafísico
y a Hegel
            tan abstracto
le resultó el asunto demasiado absoluto

Por mi parte
                    propongo al siglo XX
una hipótesis simple
que los críticos llamarán romántica
Oh muchacha que lees este poema
el mundo gira alrededor de ti

HYPOTHESIS

Ptolemy thought
                    the world was like certain women's eyes
A sphere of wet crystal
where each star traces a perfect orbit
without passion
                    tide or catastrophe

Copernicus came along
wise man who traded breasts for domes
cosines for fright
and the sun's pupil became the centre of the universe
while Giordano Bruno crackled
to the delight of husbands and priests

Then Galileo
                    probing deep into young girls' hearts
drowned in good wine
– *light gathered up by sun* –
he raped stars who were not from movies
and before he died on a comet's tail
declared love to be infinite

Kant for his part knew nothing of women
prisoner in a butterfly of calculations
in metaphysical pollen
and for Hegel
                    so abstract
the problem was excessively absolute

As for me
                    I propose to the twentieth century
a simple hypothesis
that critics will call romantic
Oh young girl who reads this poem
the world revolves about you

CON RARO OLOR A MUNDO

Acaba de llegar César Vallejo
y trae quemaduras de la guerra
roto el bastón de apalear sombras
la levita turbia
                como siempre
                        de tristeza

Acaba de llegar César Vallejo
con su esqueleto de huesos robados
y la sonrisa seca
el corazón
            un nudo de pañuelo
cuarenta años de fiebre en la mirada

Acaba de llegar César Vallejo
pregunta por el Che
                        y por los asnos
saluda a los ausentes
y comienza un poema
                    sencillamente humano

Con raro olor a mundo

WITH A STRANGE SCENT OF WORLD

César Vallejo has just arrived
and brings along war burns
his cane broken from beating shadows
his vest turbid
        as always
                from sadness

César Vallejo has just arrived
with his skeleton of stolen bones
and his dry grin
his heart
        a handkerchief knot
forty years of fever in his look

César Vallejo has just arrived
asks about Che
             and the burros
greets those absent
and begins a poem
            simply human

With a strange scent of world

EPÍLOGO

Esa tarde de julio de 1942
pudo haber sido una tarde como ésta
mas Nicola Vapsarov
– manso *cadete con la vida bajo las cejas*
marinero en las espumas de África
mecánico de árboles
poeta puro de chaqueta azul
comunista
        en fin
                con sus treintitrés años –
quiso llevarse un poco de cielo en la mirada

En el campo de tiro
de la Escuela Militar de Sofía
entre los recogidos cabellos de la lluvia
la luz de los disparos
                le reventó los ojos

Quizás el estampido le esté dando
aún vueltas al mundo
                y por eso las garzas
en las tardes
           siempre vuelan al sur
y la fiera muchacha del país de las flores
me regala ese libro del color de sus ojos
que me pone a caminar La Habana
                    como un náufrago
pensando en cómo escribir un poema
que sea traducido a treinta idiomas y empiece

La lucha es despiadadamente cruel
                necesaria

EPILOGUE

That July afternoon in 1942
could have been an afternoon like this one
and Nicola Yonkov Vapsarov
– tame *cadet with life beneath his brow*
marine in Africa's sea foam
tree mechanic
                              pure blue jacket poet
communist
              in sum
                              with his thirty three years –
wanted to carry a bit of sky in his look

But at the firing range
of Sophia's Military School
above rain's gathered hair
the dark light of gunshots
                              shattered his eyes

Perhaps the echo is still travelling
round the world
and so the herons
                    in the afternoon
always fly south
and a fierce girl from the country of flowers
gives me a book the colour of her eyes
It makes me walk around Havana
                              like I'm shipwrecked
thinking about how to write a poem

that could be translated into thirty languages and begins
Struggle is mercilessly cruel
                    necessary

II

from / de
LONELY MAN'S NEWS
NOTICIARIO DEL SOLO

ANTIPOEMA

A punto de escribir
"el estado natural del hombre es la tristeza"
te me has aparecido
                    casi resplandeciente

Pensaba continuar
                    "y todo lo que haga
será para llegar a la alegría"
mas te veo desnuda – como nunca te he visto –
pecosa delgadísima llorando

Y tal vez concluir
"lo bello es una treta de la muerte"
para besar tus huesos
y buscar en la piel
                    el sitio más feliz

Todo
        criatura
                    para quedarnos solos
al final de un poema que no engaña

ANTI-POEM

At the point of writing
"man's natural state is sadness"
you have appeared
                        almost resplendent

I thought about going on
                                "and everything he does
will be to achieve happiness"
but I see you naked – like I've never seen you –
freckled thin crying

And perhaps to end
                        "beauty is death's ruse"
to kiss your bones
and search your skin
                        for the right place

All
    to remain alone
at the end of a rhyme
                        that doesn't deceive us

NOCHES

Solo – o casi solo –
torpe pulidor de lentes
                              resfriado
con hambre y música de fondo
                                        escribo
epigramas de amor
                              que no puedo leer
ni a amigos
                    ni a extraños
                                  ni a enemigos
ni al fulano que canta o la mujer que quiero
sólo a la mesa dura
palo de corazón que me acompaña
y a estas cuatro paredes antisísmicas

Habrá quien diga
                        Racional y frío
los versos desnudos y mal cortados
ausencia de paisaje
– él que comenzó loco de paisaje –
escaso de frescura
y de imaginación y de metáforas
huérfano de lirismo
Soy
        – si me lo permiten –
encorvado aprendiz de relojero
ante la cuerda rota de este mundo
que debe dar
                    ahora mismo
                                    la hora
Y qué le voy a hacer
Aquí no caen aguaceros únicos
– con miel tibia de luz
trinos verdes de pájaros borrachos
polen mineral
                    u olor a mariposa yerta –
y ya no soy
                fatalmente

NIGHTS

Alone – or almost alone –
clumsy polisher of lenses
                    chilled
hungry and with music in the background
                                   I write
epigrams of love
                I can't read
to friends
            strangers
                    enemies
the guy singing or the woman I love
only to the rough table
hardwood accompanying me
and these four anti-seismic walls

Someone will say
                Rational and cold
naked poorly-divided verses
absence of countryside
– he who was so wild about countryside –
lacking freshness
imagination and metaphors
orphan of lyricism
I am
    – if I may –
a watchmaker's hunched-back apprentice
facing the broken watch spring of this world
that right now
                ought
                    to strike the hour
And what can I do
singular rain showers don't fall here
– with honey warm from light
green songs of drunken birds
mineral pollen
                or scent of rigid butterfly –
and I am no longer
                fatally

un niño
y falta sobre todo una mujer
que levante una llama pequeñita
y deshiele los huesos con que ardo

Sobre la mesa
                    un pomo de jarabe turbio
ceniza de espejuelos
                         centavo triste
                                    libros
llave de mí
            relojes apagados
dos lápices en cruz y una naranja negra
¿Existirás contra este mundo feo
o serás una idea
                 pluma encendida
ruido perfecto
               ángel encadenado
                                número
cierto olor imposible
o un golpe de humo azul
                     que el viento desintegra?

Aquí la noche espanta
                   Por favor amanece

                              a child
and I need most of all a woman
to raise a tiny flame
and thaw my burning bones

On the table
                    a bottle of turbid cough medicine
the remains of my glasses
                              one sad penny
                                        books
my key
        dead watches
two crossed pencils and a black orange
Might you exist against this ugly world
or are you an idea
                    enflamed feather
perfect noise
                enchained angel
                              number
certain impossible smell
or a gust of blue smoke
                        dissembled by the wind?

Here night frightens me
                        Dawn please hurry

LEYENDA

Ajka y Velo Gadevic se casaron
en 1888
Cómo
    no dice *Granma*
Temo que haría sol
               que ella llevaría
azahares en el pelo
vestido de colores muy eslavo
y él unas bombachas
             deseos y botines
Habría vino
      incienso
           pasteles y violín
– seguro al otro día amanecieron cansados
A mí
     que me casé en el malecón
con media luna y sin notario triste
no me asusta la envidia
           esa paloma negra
Ajka murió ayer – exactamente
el 12 de diciembre
de 1979
Fue un velorio moderno
Ni pésames
      ni rosarios
         ni llanto
Sólo nieve marrón
        mal tiempo en Yugoslavia
Velo
    ciento diez años – un lustro más que ella –
declaró
     Por ahora no volveré a casarme
Granma sostiene que dieron noventa y una vueltas
al sol juntos
      amándose
         sobre el mismo lecho

LEGEND

Ajka and Velo Gadevic got married
in 1888
How
     Granma doesn't report
I fear it was a sunny day
                she would have worn
orange blossoms in her hair
a colourful Slavic dress
and he a pair of peasant trousers
                       desires and high shoes
There would have been wine
              incense
                  cakes and violins –
surely they woke up tired the next morning
As for me
         I got married at the sea wall
under a half moon and without a sad justice-of-the-peace
I'm not scared by
            the black dove envy
Ajka died yesterday
– precisely on December 12th
1979
It was a modern funeral
No condolences
         rosaries
            tears
Only brown snow
           bad weather in Yugoslavia
Velo
     one hundred ten – five years older than she –
declared
        For now I will not get married again
Granma claims they circled the sun
ninety one times together
           loving each other
                in the same bed

Yo no voy a morir
pero de mí rendida
                    acaba de volar
esa paloma ciega por la nada

I'm not going to die
but that defeated dove

      has just flown away from me
blinded by nothingness

AUTORRETRATOS

He aquí el caballete
De cáñamo y lino
          el lienzo puro
tenso en el bastidor
La paleta ovalada con todos los colores
Azul de cobalto
              negro de marfil
amarillo de nápoles
Un juego de pinceles
                una espátula
y un litro de aguarrás
Sólo faltan la luz
la mano torpe
          cualquier desengaño
tu rostro *hipócrita lector* quieto

Un muro en carne viva
Cuatro palmas reales
                desdibujadas
como todas las frases de mi hijo
La línea húmeda del horizonte
El perro
        – un perro sordo
que le ladra a su sombra
Un ómnibus de humo
Todo sereno pulcro ordenado
a punto de estallar

SELF-PORTRAITS

Here you have the easel
Pure canvas
                of hemp and linen
tense on the frame
The oval board with all its colours
Cobalt blue
                marble black
Neapolitan yellow
A set of brushes
                    palette knife
and a litre of turpentine
You only need radiance
a clumsy hand
                any kind of disillusion
your still face *hypocritical reader*

A wall in the raw
Four royal palm trees
                    blurry
like everything my son says
Horizon's humid line
The dog –
            a deaf dog
barking at its shadow
A smoky bus
Everything serene tidy in order
at the point of bursting

COMPLEJO DE CULPA

¡Maldito el que crea que esto es un poema!
Jaime Sabines

Esta noche mi madre
　　　　　　se ha acostado llorando

Sus sollozos hacen carbón mi sueño
mi sueño de verdad

Sobre el costado que a veces le duele
en posición fetal
　　　　　　Zenaida Núñez gime

Mi hermano le pregunta si los nervios
si la luna menguante
　　　　　　el fogón o el Partido

Ella sólo responde
　　　　　　que le duele la vida

Y yo me voy hacia la madrugada
a conversar quizás con algún muerto

¿Quién ordena en el mundo
　　　　　　el llanto de mi madre?

GUILT COMPLEX

Damned be the one who thinks this is a poem!
Jaime Sabines

Tonight my mother
                has gone to bed crying

Her sobs turn my dreams to coal
my dreams of truth

Lying on the side that sometimes hurts
in a fetal position
                Zenaida Núñez groans

My brother asks her if it's nerves
the waning moon
                the stove burner or politics

She merely responds
                life hurts

And I leave around dawn
to talk perhaps to a dead man

Who in this world orders
                my mother's cry?

MANIFIESTO

Tengo a veces unas ganas inmensas
de abrir la ventana y dar un grito
Un grito zeppelín
con el cual remontarme
                              más allá de la muerte
Pero sucede entonces
que me da más pena conmigo mismo
pues mi ventana siempre está abierta
Además
            para qué despertar a los vecinos

Me gustaría decir
"ángeles que beben trovan fornican
en la taberna humeante
sucia de mi corazón
                        la cuenta está pagada"
Pero debo decir
"el anticomunismo
es una estrategia global de la burguesía
para seguir robándome
el vino los deseos las canciones"
Y entonces soluciono
"ángeles que beben trovan fornican
el anticomunismo
es una estrategia global de la burguesía
Ofrézcanle sus alas a la revolución"

Líricos coloquiales
                        ¿la cuenta está pagada?

MANIFESTO

At times I have an immense desire
to open the window and yell
A zeppelin yell
with which I can soar
                              beyond death
But then
I'm even more ashamed
since my window is always open
Besides
            why wake the neighbours

I would like to say
"angels drinking chanting fornicating
in the smoky dirty tavern
of my heart
                  the bill is paid"
But I ought to say
"anticommunism
is a global strategy of the bourgeoisie
to keep robbing me of
wine desire song"
And then I come up with a solution
"angels drinking chanting fornicating
anticommunism
is a global strategy of the bourgeoisie
The revolution needs your wings"

Lyrical
            colloquial
                        is the bill paid?

A PESAR DE LA LUZ

Ese olor me persigue
Pero ahora es de día
y en las aceras del Bosque de Chapultepec
los vendedores cubren sus productos con nylon
mientras se mojan firmes
Y en la Terminal Central del Poniente
los lumínicos silban
Líneas Unidas del Sur
                           Omnibus Azteca de Oro
Turismo Corona Roja

Ese olor me seduce
Pero ahora es de día
y he comido unos huevos estrellados
con tortillas y chiles
                       sobre un mantel magenta
Y he buscado mi asiento
en el 3 y 15 para Toluca
que aún está vacío
                     y solo en el andén

Ese olor ya me espanta
Pero ahora es de día
y me asombro con feas y bonitas
las montañas nevadas
los carteles que anuncian un nuevo presidente
Y no me pasmo menos con las grandes vitrinas
que devuelven el rostro a los opacos
congregados al margen
                     al filo del cristal

Hay un extraño olor lejos de casa

REGARDLESS OF THE LIGHT

This scent follows me
But now it's daytime
and on the sidewalks of Chapultepec Forest
the vendors cover their products with plastic
while they stubbornly get wet
And at the Westside Central Terminal
the lights whistle
Líneas Unidas del Sur
                    Omnibus Azteca de Oro
Turismo Corona Roja

This scent seduces me
But now it's daytime
and I've eaten fried eggs
with tortillas and chillies
                              on a magenta tablecloth
And I've looked for my seat
on the 3:15 to Toluca
still empty
              and alone at the platform

This scent frightens me
But now it's daytime
and I'm amazed by girls ugly and beautiful
the snow-covered volcanoes
the posters announcing a new president
And I'm no less astounded by large shop windows
returning to the opaque their faces
all congregated on the margin
                              the glass's edge

There is a strange scent far from home

LAMENTO POR MRS. MONES

para Roberto Méndez

Bajo el único álamo rojo que crece
en el cementerio de indigentes de Hart Island
Rita Serrano tiembla
Entre sus finas manos
que han hecho feliz a más de un hombre
ella estruja el periódico de la tarde
que todos han leído en New York City
Conrado Mones
                    de origen cubano
se suicidó introduciéndose en la jaula de los osos
en el Zoológico del Central Park
Ella no va de negro
como iría – en su lugar – la gente de Artemisa
Lleva unos blue jeans muy apretados
suéter blanco y zapatos deportivos
como en la foto de primera plana
Conrado Mones
                    – veintinueve años –
no era loco ni vagabundo ni delincuente
Era un profesor de biología
                    desempleado
El crudo otoño del 82
la envuelve la sacude casi la desnuda
para que ella no olvide las palabras
que su marido dijo
                    al guardián de los osos
Siempre es lo mismo
                    no tengo futuro
Hay que acercarse a los animales
Yo al menos trato de demostrarles que los amo
Bajo el único álamo rojo que crece
en el cementerio de indigentes de Hart Island
Rita Serrano llora
Y de sus finas manos
que han hecho sufrir a muchos hombres
                                    han caído

LAMENT FOR MRS. MONES

for Roberto Méndez

Beneath the only red poplar growing
in Hart Island's indigent cemetery
Rita Serrano trembles
In her fine hands
that have made more than one man happy
she crushes the evening paper
everyone has read in New York City
Conrado Mones
                    of Cuban origin
committed suicide by entering the bear cage
in Central Park Zoo
She is not dressed in black
as those from Artemisa – in her place – would be
She wears tight blue jeans
white sweater and tennis shoes
like the picture on the front page
Conrado Mones
                    – 29 years old –
was not crazy or homeless or criminal
He was an unemployed
                    biology professor
The crude autumn of '82
envelopes her shakes her almost undresses her
so she won't forget the words
her husband said
                    to the bear keeper
It's always the same
                    I have no future
We need to get closer to the animals
I at least try to show I love them
Beneath the only red poplar growing
in Hart Island's indigent cemetery
Rita Serrano cries
And from her fine hands
that have made many men suffer
                    has fallen

el diario de la tarde la niebla en New York City
Y nadie
          nadie en los alrededores podrá
tan lejos de Artemisa
                    consolarla

the evening paper New York City's fog
And no one
        no one around
so far from Artemisa
             can console her

NOTICIARIO DEL SOLO

para Arturo Arango

El miliciano está conversando
                      con un ángel
A las vacas que pastaban luciérnagas
en el campo de tiro
les han crecido unos cuernos de cristal rosado
Un águila picotea las nubes
                      espuma de silencio
El cuartelero silba
el querubín se espanta
                y todo huele a pólvora

Habla sola la radio
                sembrada en una piedra
—Cristiano Montarelli
chico de Trieste
        Italia
es fisiológicamente alérgico a la ropa
Y la naturaleza lo ha dotado
de un sistema de regulación térmica
que lo hace insensible
ante los cambios de temperatura

El ángel sonríe lejos
              Montado en
su pequeño helicóptero de bruma
va zurciendo las nubes
El águila está presa
              en una lágrima azul
Las vacas se desmayan de flores sin olvido
Y las luciérnagas van encendiendo los ojos
llueven alegres sobre el miliciano
como gotas de sol

—El profesor Gunar
            sabio soviético
ha podido escuchar cómo solloza
una hierba escaldada

LONELY MAN'S NEWS

for Arturo Arango

The soldier is talking
                        to an angel
At the firing range
the cows grazing on lightning bugs
have grown pink glass horns
An eagle pecks at the clouds
                        silent foam
The guard whistles
the cherub is frightened
                        and it smells like gun powder

The radio sowed in a stone
                        talks to itself –
Cristiano Montarelli
a boy from Trieste
                Italy
is physiologically allergic to clothes
Nature has endowed him
with a thermal regulation system
making him insensitive
to changes in temperature

The angel smiles from far off
                        Riding in
his tiny helicopter of mist
stitching clouds
The eagle is imprisoned
                        in a blue tear
The cows faint from flowers with no oblivion
And the eyes of lightning bugs brighten
raining happily on the soldier
like drops of sun–

Professor Gunar
                wise Soviet
has been able to hear how
a pulled weed sobs

Otras investigaciones demuestran
que puede existir un diálogo entre
hombres y vegetales
y que éstos reaccionan con espasmos
de terror cuando ante ellos se toman
actitudes violentas

Los dos imaginarias se han puesto a conversar
casi dormidos con el cuartelero
Como no ven el ángel orinar desde su
helicóptero de humo
ni las vacas que pastan luciérnagas
en el campo de tiro
ni el águila deshilando las nubes
ni una lágrima rota como un huevo
creen que va a llover se congelan y entonan
"Tú viniste a vivir y no a morir"

Other investigations demonstrate
that a dialogue between
humans and plants can exist
and that the latter suffer with spasms
of terror when violent actions
are committed in their presence

The two sleepy sentries
have begun to talk to the guard
Since they don't see the angel urinating
from his helicopter of smoke
or the cows grazing on lightning bugs
at the firing range
or the eagle shredding clouds
or a tear broken like an egg
they think it's going to rain freezing they sing in tune
"You came to live not to die"

III

from / *de*
NOBODY'S POEMS
LOS POEMAS DE NADIE

¿ARTE POÉTICA?

para María Santucho y Víctor Casaus

Saqué unos ojos miopes
                              una nariz bisiesta
unos labios que no puedo juntar
un pelo de camello
más un cuerpo de atleta retirado

También el mal genio de mi padre
el dolor en el lado de mi madre
el lunar sospechoso de mi abuela
el cólico nefrítico de todos
y hasta las fiebres constantes de mi hijo

Razones que me obligan
a tener mala opinión de la belleza

THE ART OF POETRY?

for María Santucho and Víctor Casaus

I inherited a myopic gaze
leap-year nose
lips always just slightly parted
hair of a camel
and the body of an athlete
                              retired

Then too my father's bad temper
my mother's angst
my grandmother's suspicious mole
everyone's bad kidneys
and even the frequent fevers
                          of my son

All are reason enough
to hold beauty
                    in poor esteem

A LA MEMORIA DE

Olvidaste
　　　　la escopeta de pino
que una tarde sin asma te consagró el abuelo
La ardiente barbacoa
　　　　　　　　con su molino zurdo
los peces amarillos que bebían las vacas

Olvidaste
　　　　el ciruelo parido
las tablas de maíz violadas por el norte
Y la locomotora
　　　　　　que una mañana entera
te tiznó la última camisa de la infancia

Pero no te detengas
Sólo quería recordarte que
　　　　　　　　ya sabes olvidar

TO THE MEMORY OF

You forgot
          the pine shotgun that one breathable day
your grandfather consecrated to you
The burning loft
                    with its left-handed mills
yellow fish swallowed by cows

You forgot
          the plum tree bearing fruit
the cornfields raped by the north wind
And the locomotive
                    that one morning
blackened your last shirt from childhood

But don't linger
I only wanted to remind you
                         you know how to forget

INSTANTÁNEA

Y de pronto el sillón
                    como si oyera
las primeras palabras de la lluvia
se está moviendo solo
en la esquina más lógica del cuarto
donde la luz es poca
y germinan unos zapatos viejos

Quién lo detiene ahora
después de ese relámpago
que levanta la falda a la vecina
de ese reloj dormido
desde las nueve y veinte que despierta
de este papel con flores
para ningún regalo donde escribo

Seguro de que todo es para siempre

SNAPSHOT

And suddenly the rocking chair
                                    as if hearing
rain's first words
is moving by itself
in the most logical corner of the room
where there is little light
and some old shoes germinate

Who stops it now
after a lightening bolt
lifts the neighbour's skirt
a sleeping watch
awakens at nine twenty
after the flowered wrapping paper
for no gift where I write

Sure that everything is forever

CAYAMA REVISITED

Todos los viajes, todos mis
viajes, son viajes de regreso
León de Greiff

Algo cruje detrás de las palabras Bien puede ser la luna enganchada en un gajo de Dios que vomita un hilo de araña sin desanudar Bien el cernícalo de niebla que se estrella contra la frente de mi madre tras las abejas de la medianoche O bien el ladrido inconfundible de las espigas inflamadas y las flores recién poseídas por el rocío

Pero a todos importan las doradas cenizas Barrio que ha dormido en mí y que abandona sus huevos de cristal sobre las nubes que brotan de las brasas del silencio Silencio como lluvia soleada que no ha caído aún pero que espera detrás del aromal una seña ya dada por el ahogo del abuelo Abuelo que avanza con el machete en ristre hacia el espejo es decir contra la nada

Hilo que robé a mi abuela y que era puro como la sangre de las adelfas que no trovan desde ayer Que robé a tía Güisa y estaba turbio y no sirvió para empinar el cielo Que robé a tía Cuca y era débil porque estaba anudado entre las vísceras del pluviómetro Que robé a mi madre y no reventará aunque tire de él la primavera Algo cruje detrás de las palabras

Por aquí anda mi casa y juro ante Dios no haberla vendido ni extraviado en la caligrafía del camino Con sus once pupilas de madera para el viento de octubre que le desempolva el alma y rompe los vitrales del silencio La casa que habita en mí y que protejo de las tormentas en celo y de los soles asesinos Pero a todos importan las doradas cenizas

CAYAMA REVISITED

All journeys, all my
journeys, are return journeys
León de Greiff

Something creaks behind the words Perhaps it is the moon hanging from a branch of God vomiting a disentangled spider's web Fog's kestrel shattering against my mother's forehead behind midnight's bees Or the unmistakable barking of enflamed tassels and flowers recently possessed by dew

But golden ashes are important to everyone Neighbourhood that has slept in me and abandons its glass eggs on clouds sprouting from silence's hot coals Silence like sunned rain not yet fallen but waiting behind the *marabú* a signal already given by Grandpa's shortness of breath Grandpa advancing with his machete raised towards the mirror or against nothing

Thread I stole from my Grandma pure like the blood of oleanders singing out of tune since yesterday That I stole from Aunt Güisa turbid and won't work for raising the sky That I stole from Aunt Cuca weak because it was knotted among the rain gauge's viscera That I stole from my mother and won't break even if spring is dragged with it Something creaks behind the words

Around here is my house and I swear to God I haven't sold or misplaced it on the road's calligraphy With its eleven wood pupils for October's wind dusting off its soul and breaking the windowpanes of stillness The house that lives in me and I protect from storms in heat and from assassin suns But golden ashes are important to everyone

SONETO NEGRO

Conozco este silencio
por ese inconfundible olor a estrella
Este silencio a gritos de las cosas
que no pueden durar

¿Quiénes son los que yacen
en las abiertas tumbas de mi sueño?
¿Habrán entrado en ti
al ser desenterrados por la lluvia?

Es la hora del otro
la que marca el reloj de las abejas
Ya se inicia el comercio de las almas

¿Por qué la luna brilla
tan sólo en la mirada de esos muertos?
¿Yo soy el que revive?

BLACK SONNET

I know this silence
by the definite scent of stars
This screaming silence of things
that cannot last

Who are those who lie
in the open tombs of my dreams?
Have they entered you
upon being unearthed by rain?

It is the other's hour
shown by bees' watch
The commerce of souls is about to begin

Why does the moon glow
only in the glance of those dead?
Is it I who will live once more?

VILLANCICO

Vean
    es un árbol de navidad
que creció sin dolor
        y sin campanas
en la esquina más densa de la noche

Cierta la falsa nieve
que florece en sus gajos
las guirnaldas que duran apenas un invierno
la estrella de oropel
        allá en la copa

Vean
    es un árbol de navidad
pues en él
      como un péndulo
se columpia la lumbre del ahorcado

CHRISTMAS CAROL

There is a Christmas tree
painlessly growing
                        without bells
in night's densest corner

The false snow
flowering in its boughs
the garlands hardly lasting one winter
the tinsel star way on top
                        are all real

It is a Christmas tree
for there
            like a pendulum
the hanged man's brilliance sways

INGENIERÍA NAVAL

La estrella del timón
                        recién cortada
del jardín de la noche
Ese casco
            con algo de violín
que ha perdido las cuerdas
El mástil que florece
relámpagos
                        entre nubes naranjas
Todo cruje en el barco
que ha pintado mi hijo

Para mi padre
                el capitán
                            escribo barcos
¿Será mi padre ese sueño que tuve
cuando dormí en Cayama
con la pequeña almohada de mi madre?
Ellos son de papel
pero sólo naufragan
                        cuando no arde la tinta

Barcos que vienen
                    del fondo del océano
Barcos que van
a los puertos del cielo
Barcos sin rumbo fijo
                        de la nada a la nada

NAVAL ENGINEERING

The wheel's star
                    freshly cut
from night's garden
The hull
            evokes a violin
that's lost its strings
The mast blooms lightning
among orange clouds
Everything creaks in this boat
my son has painted

For my father
                the captain
                                I write boats
Might my father be the dream I had
when I slept in Cayama
upon my mother's tiny pillow?
They are made of paper
and wreck only
                    when not inflamed by ink

Boats rising
                from ocean's floor
Boats docking
at the gates of heaven
Aimless boats
                sailing from nowhere to nothing

HAPPY BIRTHDAY

Cuando ya todo se aleja de mí
y entro en la desmemoria
ese cielo disonante
               sin odio
como un astro perdido

Cuando ya todo se aleja de ti
y de ese inconfundible
penetrante olor a nada que brota
de tu pelvis
          estrella desmentida

Cuando ya todo se aleja de todo
y la menor distancia
que late entre dos puntos
es lo que nos desune
              he vuelto a arder

Ceniza de infinito

HAPPY BIRTHDAY

When everything is far from me
and I enter in forgetfulness
that inharmonic sky
                 without hate
like a lost celestial body

When everything is far from you
and the unmistakable
incisive scent of nothing
sprouting from your pelvis
                  refuted star

When everything is far from everything
and the smallest distance
pounding between two points
is what separates us
               I start to burn again

The infinite's ash

CONTRASEÑA

A la entrada del Báltico
te esperan las gaviotas

El agua será oscura
como uno de tus sueños sin verano
La costa será clara
     como nada de mí

A la entrada del Báltico
Allí las dejé yo

El cielo estará cerca
casi podrás tocarlo con mis dedos
El barco se alejará
     como nada de ti

Guarda la contraseña
Todo buen corazón es un prismático

COUNTERSIGN

At the entrance to the Baltic
                              seagulls await you

The water will be obscure
like one of your summerless dreams
The coast will be clear
                              like nothing that is mine

I left them there
at the entrance to the Baltic

The sky will descend
with my fingers you can almost touch it
The ship will fade away
                              like nothing that is yours

Keep the countersign safe
Every good heart is a telescope

JAM SESSION
para Sinnica Jacq

Con esa batería
el sol sale de noche en su jardín

Con ese contrabajo
la babosa saluda al pájaro carpintero

Con ese saxofón
el lagarto descubre las estrellas

Con esa tumbadora
el lirio pide amor a la cizaña

Con ese piano forte
la mariposa vuelve por fin a su capullo

Y con esa trompeta
                    se está riendo Dios

JAM SESSION

for Sinnica Jacq

With those drums
sun rises at night in its garden

With that bass
the slug greets the woodpecker

With that saxophone
the lizard discovers stars

With that conga
the lily asks for thistle's love

With that piano
the butterfly finally returns to its cocoon

And with that trumpet
                    God laughs

POEMA CON GORRIONES

para Pável Grushkó

Por mi ventana entran los gorriones
que no saben volar
Yo les ofrezco uñas
ideas fermentadas
          migajitas de espanto

Brilla el doble cristal de los domingos

Por mi ventana entran los gorriones
que no saben volar
Yo les ofrezco pecas
esta memoria áspera
          cascaritas de angustia

Sólo falta a Moscú
          las hojas de los árboles

Por mi ventana entran los gorriones
que no saben volar
Yo les ofrezco dientes
una música oscura
          semillas de ansiedad

¿De qué parte del cielo será el vino?

POEM WITH SPARROWS

for Pável Grushkó

Through my window enter sparrows
not knowing how to fly
I offer them fingernails
fermented ideas
                crumbs of dread

Sundays' double pane shines

Through my window enter sparrows
not knowing how to fly
I offer them freckles
this rough memory
                husks of anguish

Moscow only lacks
                the leaves of its trees

Through my window enter sparrows
not knowing how to fly
I offer them teeth
a dark music
                seeds of anxiety

From what part of the sky
                comes wine?

SUITE DE SELVA NEGRA

para Gloria e Iván Kauffmann

En Selva Negra cae
                    un agua sin dolor
El liquen de los árboles
nos da las buenas noches
Vamos entre la niebla
y estoy seguro que nos perderemos

Kalia
        hada del bosque
                        acompáñanos
En medio del camino hacia la noche
la coral resplandece
Acompáñanos
                Loscar
                        duende de la montaña

Las nubes – ellas sí
cumplieron su promesa
Han cubierto los cerros
verdes como los ojos
de mi antigua nostalgia
En el lago
            los cisnes
casi nada prometen
Cantan cosas estúpidas
como toda belleza

Hay otra Selva Negra
                    más allá de esta lluvia
que corre entre las piedras
enlodadas del alma
Hay otra Selva Negra
                    más allá de esta angustia
que salta por los pinos
como una ardilla roja

Zenaida está temblando

BLACK FOREST SUITE

for Gloria and Iván Kauffmann

In Black Forest
                    water falls painlessly
The tree lichen
bids us goodnight
We move in mist
and I know we will lose our way

Kalia
        wood fairy
                        come with us
Halfway towards night
the coral snake gleams
Come with us
                    Loscar
                            mountain elf

The clouds did
                        keep their promise
They have covered the hills
green as the eyes
of my ancient nostalgia
On the lake
                    swans
promise almost nothing
They sing only stupidities
like all that is beautiful

There is another Black Forest
                                beyond this rain
running among stones
muddied with soul
There is another Black Forest
                                beyond this anguish
leaping like a red squirrel
from pine to pine

Zenaida trembles

y se ha quedado atrás
Sentada en una piedra
donde blasfema el río
Le acompaña el Enano
que dejó de llorar
Ambos se calentaron
con aquel mismo cuento

Ya la luna chismea con los monos
Ya la niebla
              comienza a retoñar
Ya las rosas asustan a los niños

Mi bien
        en Selva Negra
se derrama la noche
                gota a gota
Y todo huele a luna
a maderas preciosas
a música
            a pasado
Mi bien
        en Selva Negra
no deja de llover
pero el agua nos grita como el fuego

      and lingers
She sits on a rock
where the river curses
The Dwarf sits with her
and stops crying
They warm themselves
with that same story

Now the moon gossips with monkeys
The mist
      begins to return
Roses frighten children

My love
      in Black Forest
night overflows
          drop by drop
And everything smells of moon
the finest woods
music
    long ago
My love
      in Black Forest
it rains endlessly
but the water calls out to us like fire

DRAMA DE MARCO POLO

para Margaret Randall

Algo he visto del mundo
Las tormentas de polvo de Managua
la nieve ya desnuda
en los pinares del camino a Smolyan
y cómo discuten las banderas en la torre
de la Universidad de Puerto Rico

Algo he visto del mundo
Las piedras encantadas de Palenque
la bahía de miel
que olvidó el verano en Ponta Delgada
y aquella Plaza Roja
pintada por Kandinsky

Algo he visto del mundo
y eso ahonda mi pena
                    Nada me pertenece

MARCO POLO'S DILEMMA

for Margaret Randall

I've seen something of the world
Managua's dust storms
the bare snow
on the pines along the road to Smolyan
and the flags arguing atop the tower
of the University of Puerto Rico

I've seen something of the world
Palenque's bewitched stones
the bay of honey
forgotten by summer at Ponta Delgada
and the Red Square
                      Kandinsky painted

I've seen something of the world
and it only heightens my pain
Nothing belongs to me

POEMA POR EMILY

para Ramón Fernández-Larrea

Emily Dickinson
                la ranita de Amherst
que croaba en las piedras
cuando la luna negaba al saltamontes
no conoció el mar
Y sin embargo dijo
Ya ni los niños preguntan
Sólo las olas contestan

Emily Dickinson
                la abejita de New England
que libaba en las noches
el zumo helado de las estrellas
no supo de montañas
Y sin embargo dijo
El cielo es todo aquello que no puedo alcanzar
Mi fe es mayor que las colinas

Emily Dickinson
                el pajarito yanqui
que jamás tuvo nido
ni vio quebrarse el huevo del orgasmo
Y sin embargo dijo
                Soy esposa
Si consigo evitar
que un corazón se rompa

No habré vivido en vano

POEM FOR EMILY

for Ramón Fernández Larrea

Emily Dickinson
                     tiny Amherst frog
croaking among the stones
when the moon denied grasshoppers
never knew the sea
Still she said
And the children no further question
And only the waves reply

Emily Dickinson
                     tiny New England bee
who by night sipped
the frozen nectar of stars
never knew mountains
Still she said
Heaven is what I cannot reach
My faith is larger than the hills

Emily Dickinson
                     tiny Yankee bird
never had a nest
nor shattered the yellow shell of orgasm
Still she said
               I'm wife
If I can stop one heart from breaking

I shall not live in vain

A VER SI ME EXPLICO

para Eduardo Heras León

Poesía es algo en realidad posible si prescindimos de las palabras La ausencia de color mejor dicho la luz con que los astros se saludan El reposo no el movimiento y por tanto la danza coagulada El escenario abandonado por los comediantes la obra que ve cada noche el tramoyista El silencio y no la música – esa herida por donde todo se desangra El relámpago contra la pantalla cuando Dios hace el cambio de bobina José Martí con el grillete y no la piedra en medio de la Plaza

Poesía es estar sentado ante esta mesa y escribir con letras azules la palabra *poesía* El viento que viene del lago y que refresca la noche de carbón encendido de Managua Descubrirse los ganglios inflamados y mañana tener que madrugar para los análisis El relámpago del tren y el trueno del avión o sea el anuncio de cualquier partida Haber cumplido treinta y tres años e intuir los centuriones los clavos y la cruz La carta en que mi hijo me dice que *creo boy a hacer de tu tamaño*

Poesía es el sentido de mi vida lo que poco importa pues estos son los poemas de nadie

LET'S SEE IF I CAN EXPLAIN MYSELF
for Eduardo Heras León

Poetry is something actually possible if we disregard words The absence of colour better said the light stars use to greet one another Rest not movement and so coagulated dance The stage abandoned by performers the play seen each night by stagehands Silence and not music –the wound from where everything bleeds Lightening bolt against the screen when God changes the reels José Martí with shackles and not the stone in the middle of the Plaza

Poetry is sitting at this table and marking in blue letters the word *poetry* The wind coming off the lake to cool the burning carbon of night in Managua Discovering my glands are swollen and tomorrow having to get up early for lab tests Train's lightening and aeroplane's thunder or rather the announcement of any kind of departure Having turned thirty three and sensing the centurions the nails the cross The letter where my son says *i think i'm gonna bee as tall as u*

Poetry is my life's sense and it matters little for these are nobody's poems

IV

from / *de*
THE LAST TO THE FAIR
EL ÚLTIMO A LA FERIA

HOSPITALES

De la mano de quién
los enfermos del Pabellón Yarini
van a desayunar
como cada mañana de su muerte
Los pijamas rosados
casi sin excepción
                    les quedan cortos
entallados al cuerpo que se niega a vivir
Ellos beben con prisa
de la leche caliente que les sirve
solfeando
                ese negrito que se pinta solo
El prócer de la salubridad pública
desde el oscuro mármol
                            los mira muy atento
mas sin sombra de conmiseración

De la mano de quién
los enfermos del Pabellón Yarini
van a desayunar
Como cada mañana de su muerte
Detrás de ellos
                el polvo
agolpado en la luz
                        avanza en procesión
Los árboles se asoman
sin curiosidad a los ventanales
cerrados hoy
                ante el falso invierno de la isla
Y la jefa de sala
                demorada y fulgente
hace su entrada de última
con una gran nostalgia entre las piernas

Todo ascenso es inevitable

HOSPITALS

Who leads
the sick of Pavilion Yarini
to breakfast
like each morning of their death
Pink pyjamas
almost without exception
                          are too short
fitted to their bodies refusing to live
They quickly swallow
                          warm milk served by
an over-the-top black kid
                          solfaing
Public health's national hero
watches them attentively
without a bit of commiseration

Who leads
the sick of Pavilion Yarini
to breakfast
Like each morning of their death
Behind them dust
crowded in light
                          advances in procession
Trees appear
incuriously at the large windows
closed today
                          before the island's false winter
And the charge nurse
                          slow and radiant
makes her entrance last
with a great nostalgia between her legs

All ascension is inevitable

NUBES

Algazara de nubes
que no me dejan ver
                    la piel de toro herido
Luces que se saludan
quizás sin recordarse
Meseta castellana
árida como estos versos
                    al fin

Sólo le vi los ojos
                    madre cerrada en luto
por el pañuelo blanco
Capricho de las nubes
enmudecer el cielo de la página
Mansos ojos de Ulises
                    que tejía y destejía
como fiera Penélope

Yo no duermo
                    vigilo
las nubes del desierto
que se embarcan en el Mediterráneo
Ni una sola isla por testigo
Sólo el rastro de sol
que no siguen las naves ni mi alma
marinera de espacios

Y de repente
            África
Sombras que se entrecruzan
como densos relámpagos
Las líneas de la tarde
enredando lo azul
En la bolsa
            vomitaré palabras

No vuelvas a confiar en la belleza

CLOUDS

Clouds' clamour
not letting me see
                    a wounded bull's hide
Lights greet one another
perhaps not remembering
Castilian plateau
arid like my verses
                    at last

I only saw her eyes
                    mother enclosed in mourning
by a white handkerchief
Clouds' whim
to silence sky on a page
Ulysses' tame look
                    knitting and unravelling
like wild Penelope

I do not sleep
but watch over desert clouds
embarking on the Mediterranean
Not one island as witness
Only the sun's sign
that neither ships nor my soul
mariner of spaces
                    follow

And suddenly
                    Africa
Shadows interlace
like dense lightening bolts
The afternoon's lines
entangle the blue
Into the bag
                    I vomit words

Never trust beauty again

CANTINA EN COCHABAMBA
o 'Llorando se fue'

Algo debes saber ya de la vida
pues la tercera ronda
siempre pone las cosas en su sitio
O pagas o te quedas
                    acodado en la barra
que a alguna hora tiene que cerrar

Lo más lejos que irás
si logras hacerte amigo de casa
será a contemplar desde tu rincón
cómo los dependientes
se entregan al balance
                    y apartan su propina

En la calle inocente
que ganaron las sombras
                    nadie espera por ti
– salvo el policía salvo el ladrón
Y cada uno de ellos
tratará de engañarte a su manera

Algo debes saber ya de la vida
Mejor es irse a tiempo
no discutir con nadie
dejar las cuentas claras
Y ver si ya está abierta
                    esa otra cantina

CANTINA IN COCHABAMBA
or 'Llorando se fue'

Something you should know of life
since the third round
puts things in perspective
You pay or you stay
                    leaning against the bar
that has to close sometime

The most you can hope for
if you become a regular
is to contemplate from your corner
employees
absorbed in balancing
                    and recounting their tips

In the innocent street
won over by shadows
                    no one awaits you –
except police except thieves
And each tries to mislead you
in their own way

Something of life you should know
Better to leave quick
not pick a fight
leave a clean tab
and see if that other cantina
                    is still open

UNA Y OTRA VEZ

A los 68 años
mi madre no tiene dónde vivir
Y no porque sea huérfana
ama de casa comunista viuda
Todo se lo destruyen a mi madre
La infancia
    el sillón de tejer
        el matrimonio
Vean cómo se asoma a los postigos
que no pudrió la lluvia
sino su propia tos
     y las ajenas lágrimas
La vida de mi madre
sin un solo beso a contraluz
sin herencia
    ni casualidad bendita
Y sobre todo
    sin final feliz
Sin un buen epitafio con la sangre
del peor de sus hijos

ONCE AND AGAIN

At sixty-eight
my mother has no place to live
And not because she is an orphan
housewife communist widow
All that is my mother's has been destroyed
Her childhood
                  the rocker where she knits
                                  marriage
Look how she peers through the shutters
not rotted by rain
but by her cough
                  distant tears
My mother's story
without a single kiss against the light
legacy
        or blessed chance
And above all
              no happy ending
not one good epitaph writ in the blood
of the least of her sons

EL CAPITÁN

Llegué tarde aquel día
que para ti era el último
Lo pensé demasiado
en mi celda del Piso Diecisiete
Pero luego te busqué con afán
entre los muertos tibios de la noche

De ti
        no guardo nada
salvo la foto de carnet descolorida
que alguna de mis primas panaderas
se arrancó para mí
Por ti
        no he derramado
en estos treinta octubres
de mi mala memoria
ni rastros de una lágrima

Y sólo llegué a tiempo
para echar a perder la ceremonia
Las campanas doraban
                        el polvo de las calles
Un viento sin sentido
encrespaba las cosas
Y las casitas viejas
                    se volvieron canción
Tan sólo llegué a tiempo
para hacer esta crónica
Y no he vuelto a la tumba

Nunca creí que me parecería
a ese viejo borracho
que acabó con la vida de mi madre
Pero ahora descubro
que sus ojos perdidos son mis ojos
pues lo único que puedo reclamar como mío

THE CAPTAIN

I arrived late the day
that would be your last
I pondered too long
in my cell on the seventeenth floor
But later I looked for you urgently
among night's still-warm dead

I have
        nothing of yours
but a faded ID picture
one of my baker cousins
halfheartedly gave me
For you
        these thirty Octobers
of my bad memory
I have not shed
even the shadow of a tear

I only arrived in time
to spoil the ceremony
The bells gilded
                the dust of these streets
A senseless wind
made everything stand on end
And the old shacks
                turned to song
I only arrived in time
to write this chronicle
And I haven't been back to your grave

I never thought I'd take after
the old drunk
who ruined my mother's life
but now I see
his lost eyes are mine
and the only thing I can claim as my own

son los labios que siempre aborrecí
Esos que tal vez para castigarme
están en la sonrisa de sus nietos

Cómo relegar aquellas hormigas
tan hambrientas de nada
Bajo el cristal
            el rostro
que debía besar
                profanado por Dios
Esas hormigas de la madrugada
preguntaban por mí

No te debo la vida
Yo también soy una casualidad
Pude crecer sin ti
– prescindiendo del maldito dinero
de un padre sin dinero
Y no me arrepiento
de haberte negado tres veces en el camino
de Casilda a Cayama
No te debo la muerte
¿Para qué me llamaste?

are the lips I always hated
those that perhaps to punish me
show in the smiles of his grandchildren

How to banish those ants
so hungry for nothing
Beneath the coffin glass
                    the face
I ought to have kissed
                    profaned by God
Daybreak's ants
asked for me

I do not owe you my life
I too am a coincidence
I grew up without you
did without the wretched money
of a penniless father
I am not sorry
I denied you three times on the road
from Casilda to Cayama
I don't owe you my death
Why did you call me?

NOCTURNO DE TRÍPOLI

No tengo más que la noche desnuda
al rojo vivo
               rociada ante mí

Su musgo está creciendo
a la vista de nadie
Lo abonan con silencio
esas horas que no quieren pasar

Mordería con sus dientes
los grandes pechos de agua
Buscaría con sus manos
el camino a la estrella
Y con su lengua robaría la sal

El musgo de la noche
se ha prendido a los muros
de este juicio sin ley
de esta angustia sin Dios

Ya me abrazo
               en la hoguera de sombras
Ya me afila la noche sentada sobre mí

TRIPOLI NOCTURNE

I have nothing more than the naked night
fiery hot
       dewed before me

Her moss grows
in the sights of no one
These hours reluctant to pass
nourish it silently

I would bite with her teeth
water's great breasts
With her hands
look for the way to Alderaban
And with her tongue steal salt

Night's moss
has taken root on the walls
of lawless trial
of Godless anguish

I burn
      in shadows' blaze
Night hones me beneath her

NOCTURNO DE MADRID

Esta noche no me promete nada
su color es jamás
Me lo dicen los huesos
                    que comienzan a arder
empapados de insomnio

Te palpo con los dedos de la noche
celaje sin pezones
                    irradiación sin labios
Y a mi almohada suben
                    despeinadas
                              las estrellas

Ya la noche
          oh relámpago puro
se derrama por mí
Y hasta los pies
              astros desorbitados
quieren dejar sus huellas en el cielo

La noche abre las piernas
y entonces yo le ofrendo
                    mi sueño fermentado
La noche sabe a nunca
                    pero huele a mañana

MADRID NOCTURNE

Tonight promises me nothing
its colour is nevermore
My bones
        beginning to ache
drenched in insomnia tell me

With night's fingers I touch you
clouds without breasts
                mouthless clarity
And unkempt stars
           climb
              my pillow

Now the night
         oh pure lightning flash
overflows for me
And even our feet
        wild stars
want to leave their prints on the sky

Night opens her legs
and I offer her
        my fermented dream
Night tastes of never
           but smells of tomorrow

A VECES

¿Se podrá por estas angostas
húmedas escaleras
llegar hasta algún sitio?
¿Ascender hasta el negro
corazón de la nieve
bajar hasta la lumbre de la piedra?

A la vida no le preguntes nada
Ella nunca responde
La vida es sorda
                              es muda
Y aunque ve por tus ojos
tú eres el sabor
                              y es ella la que palpa
A la vida no le respondas todo
Ella sólo pregunta

AT TIMES

Do these damp
            and narrow stairs
lead someplace?
Rise to snow's
            black heart
or descend to stone's brightness?

Don't ask life anything
She never answers
Life is deaf
          mute
And although she sees through your eyes
you are taste
          and it is she who touches
Do not answer life
She only asks

MITOMANÍA

Verdad es el lagarto la canasta de lirios el revólver La verdad como la envidia está en todas partes Hasta en el cielo donde se pelean los astros La verdad es la única sombra que no ciega Pregúntenle al que sangra por un puñal de nieve Verdad es la yema el alba el framboyán la nube Como el triángulo la verdad es roja Y callo pues ya he dicho demasiadas mentiras

Si dices la verdad te quedas solo Hasta Tritón la luna de Neptuno bien podría no ser un mundo inerte y estar toda cubierta con volcanes de hielo y escarcha de nitrógeno He dicho la verdad y me arrepiento Hasta el propio Neptuno bien podría tener su campo magnético inclinado y mostrar sus auroras fragantes no en los polos sino en el ecuador No me dejen mentir

La verdad ante todo Aunque cueste Como mi madre la verdad es ingenua No hay moral sin verdad Aunque cueste la vida Sin verdad no amanece Y como yo la verdad es inmadura No hay arte sin verdad Aunque cueste Sin verdad no hay sentido Como mis hijos la verdad es inocente No hay amor sin verdad Aunque cueste la muerte La verdad ante todo Jamás olvides esta gran mentira

MYTHOMANIA

Truth is the lizard a basket of lilies the revolver Truth like envy is everywhere Even in heaven where the stars do battle Truth is the only shadow that doesn't blind Ask the one bleeding from a dagger of snow Truth is a yoke the dawn a flamboyant the cloud Like the triangle truth is red And I'll quiet now that I've told so many lies

If you tell the truth you will be alone Even Triton Neptune's moon might not be an idle world but covered instead with volcanoes of ice and nitrogen frost I've told the truth and now I'm sorry Even Neptune's magnetic field might be tilted showing those fragrant auroras at its equator instead of its poles Don't let me lie

Truth above all At whatever cost Truth is candid like my mother Without truth there is no morality Though it cost us our lives Without truth there is no dawn And truth is immature like me No art without truth At whatever cost Without truth there is no sense Truth is innocent like my sons No love without truth Though it cost us our death Truth above all Never forget this enormous lie

SON NICA I

para Tomás Borge

Perdido en el país
                donde llaman invierno
a la más delirante primavera
Y donde todo cambia de verdad
gobiernos y paisajes
y los volcanes terminan sus noches
convertidos en lagos
Yo he visto
                no en la peor esquina
de la ciudad fantasma
sonrientes
                a los niños más viejos del mundo

Perdido en el país
                donde los insectos
enloquecen a las computadoras
Y donde los crepúsculos
                        flameantes
palidecen de envidia
ante el corazón de una pitajaya
Yo he visto
                no los jardines
sino los huesos florecer
bajo la luna roja
                del más crudo verano

SON NICA I

for Tomás Borge

Misplaced in the country
                    where they call
the most delirious spring
                    winter
And where everything really does change
landscapes and governments
and the volcanoes end their nights
transformed to lakes
I have seen not in the worst corner
of this ghost city
smiling
          the oldest children in the world

Misplaced in the country
                    where insects
drive computers mad
And where flaming
                    twilight
pales with envy
before the heart of strawberry pear
I have seen
          not gardens
but bones flower
beneath the red moon
                    of the cruelest summer

SON NICA 2

Tardes de Nicaragua
en que un oscuro sol
ha ofendido a los plátanos
En que una puerta cruje
pelea con el aire
casi con sentimiento
En que una vieja lapa
ha deshilado un mango
con mañas de filóloga
Y en que todo fermenta
hasta la poesía
en el congelador

Bajo un cielo de polvo
espero la serpiente
La que debe morderme
la que me salvará

SON NICA 2

Nicaraguan evenings
where a dark sun
has offended the plantains
Where a door creaks
struggles with air
almost with feeling
Where an old macaw
has unravelled a mango
with a philologist's skills
And where everything ferments
even poetry
in the freezer

Beneath a dust sky
I await the serpent
that ought to bite
that will save me

DESAYUNO CON ÁNGELES

para Claribel Alegría

Sobre la mesa
            larga y amarilla
donde posa toda la Casa Seis
El tazón de café
                y los claveles

Así lo dispusieron
Doña Leo y Dios
                ese gran matrimonio
del que soy hijo único
sin ser ni posesivo ni malcriado

(El ha atendido
                todas mis plegarias
y ella le da palos a mis camisas
para enmendarme de los muchos pecados
casi siempre mortales)

El café me hace
                sus señales de humo
Yo lo cubriré con esa crema
hecha de insomnio
                que es su negación

Los claveles
            ¿cómo decirles algo
realmente digno sobre los claveles?
Sobre todo si están recién cortados
si no los salvaré

BREAKFAST WITH ANGELS

for Claribel Alegría

On the table
                infinite and yellow
where House Number 6 poses
The coffee mug
               and carnations

This is how they arranged it
Doña Leo and God
              that great marriage
of which I'm the only child
without being possessive or spoiled

(He has answered
              all my prayers
and she has beaten my shirts with branches
to emend many of my
almost always mortal sins)

The coffee makes
              smoke signals
I will cover it with cream
made of insomnia
              its denial

The carnations
             how to say something
really dignified about carnations?
Above all if they are recently cut
if I will not save them

HABLANDO SOLO

Será posible esta conversación
llana
     con el silencio
Y sin que medien luces
               tintas de todo
Será posible esta conversación
que tal vez sólo oye
            el viento sordo
Que no quede ni rastro
ni la palabra polvo en una copa
Será posible esta conversación
sin interlocutores
           ni testigos
Como decir
       entre la nada y nadie

Todas las voces son aquella voz
que nunca has escuchado
La voz de las estrellas desveladas
La voz azul del polvo y del agua caída
La voz del musgo que se ha vuelto piedra
La voz del arco iris y el relámpago
Todas las voces son aquella voz
que calla en tus palabras

SPEAKING ALONE

Could it be possible
this plain conversation
                 with silence
And without lights smeared with all
                       mediating
Could it be possible
this conversation
that perhaps only
             deaf wind hears
That neither sign
nor the word dust remain in a glass
Could it be possible
this conversation without partner
                    or witness
Like saying
          between nothingness and no one

All voices are that voice
you have never heard
The voice of watchful stars
The blue voice of dust and fallen water
The voice of moss turned to stone
The voice of rainbow and lightning
All voices are that voice
quieting in your words

V

from / de
CEASELESS PRAYER
ORACIÓN INCONCLUSA

ENTRADA

No sé por qué camino
pero he llegado aquí
Hasta este raro sitio
sin casas ni paisaje
Este lugar desnudo
de las piedras al alma
donde el mundo germina

Quizás también tú llegas
siguiendo ese camino
En esta vida harta
de aciertos y certezas
sólo el error nos une
La poesía es el reino
de los equivocados

ENTRANCE

I do not know by which path
but I have arrived here
To this strange spot
with no houses or countryside
This naked place
from stones to soul
where the world takes root

Perhaps you too arrive
following that path
In this life sated
with success and certainties
only error unites us
Poetry is the kingdom
of the mistaken

ABISMOS

Vivo entre dos abismos
                    La paciencia
del que ya anduvo tal vez demasiado
y se acoda en el puente
– única ceremonia de la tarde –
a ver pasar las aguas
Y la impaciencia enorme
del que quiere seguir a toda costa
pero sólo ve el raudal de insomnios
y del puente se lanza
                    a tu regazo

ABYSSES

I remain amid two abysses
                          The patience
of one who has perhaps walked too long
and leans on the bridge
– evening's lone ceremony –
to see water pass
And the infinite impatience
of one who must go on at any price
yet only sees insomnia's torrent
and from the bridge throws himself
                          to your lap

BOGOTANO

para Gustavo Adolfo Garcés

Yo juego fútbol con mis asesinos
Les disputo el balón
                    gano tiempo y espacio
arriesgo esta jugada individual

Arracimados
            sobre el pasto tenaz
de este parque escogido
los gamines se sacuden el polvo
que Dios echó en su alma
                        y se bañan con sol
El de ruana molida
                busca en la bolsa plástica
el aliento de la felicidad
Y el que tiene las costillas al aire
caza como un gorrión
migajitas de pan entre la hierba

Yo juego fútbol con mis asesinos
me pasaron la bola
                y pruebo el arco
Hay más niebla en los huesos que en las calles

BOGOTANO

for Gustavo Adolfo Garcés

I play soccer with my assassins
dispute with them the ball

                     save time and space
risk this lone move

Clustered together

                over the tenacious grass
of this chosen field
the gamins shake off the dust
God cast on their souls

                and with the sun bathe
The one in a tattered poncho
searches for a breath of happiness
in a plastic bag
And the one with his ribs stuck out
hunts like a sparrow
among the blades for bread crumbs

I play soccer with my assassins
they passed the ball to me

              and I try for a goal
There is more mist in their bones than in the streets

PARAGUAS

para Alberto Restrepo

Bajo una lluvia ajena que no lo deja arder
este hombre camina
Nadie en el país del tal vez mañana
lo distingue
              con la angustia por fuera
Todos marchan deprisa hacia ese sitio donde
él muchas veces quisiera llegar
Hoy no
          pues sólo anhela
intimar con la lluvia que lo ignora
Aunque le cueste tanto como salir desnudo
el haberse puesto el alma al revés

En el alba
              los mendigos también se saludan
El negro que duerme con su perrito
le da los buenos días
al que empuja la carroza de tablillas
Y el que robó
              le ofrece una naranja
al de bufanda persa

Hoy le duele la luz
                    al extranjero
Sientan aquí su horror
a la pantalla azul
                    donde siempre es de día
El extranjero se planta y murmura
– La igualdad
              antes que la diferencia
Son ateas las noches
y el sol nos ilumina con sus manchas
Se reverencia
              a los irreverentes

UMBRELLAS

for Alberto Restrepo

Beneath an alien rain not letting him burn
this man walks
No one in the country of perhaps tomorrow
notices him
          with his anguish untucked
They all move hurriedly toward the place where
very often he would like to arrive
Today no
          since he only longs
to be friendly with the rain ignoring him
Although putting his soul on backwards
is as difficult as leaving home naked

At dawn
          the beggars too greet each another
The one sleeping with his dog
says good morning
to the one pushing his wooden cart
And the one who stole
              offers an orange
to the one with a Persian scarf

Today light hurts
          the foreigner
Feel his horror here
on the blue screen
          where it's always daytime
The foreigner makes a stand and mutters–
Equality
        before difference
Nights are atheists
and the sun illuminates us with its spots
The irreverent
         are revered

145

FRENTE FRÍO
para Hugo Luis Sánchez

Se cumple al fin el sueño de Casal
Cae nieve en La Habana

Y en la Plaza de la Revolución
hay una multitud de robustos abetos
cubiertos de guirnaldas

Haciendo realidad un acuerdo
del Comité Central
los arbolitos de navidad han florecido

Nuestro verde monótono
ha quedado como Julián quería
salpicado de blanco

Todo sueño se cumple
La Habana cae en la nieve

COLD FRONT

for Hugo Luis Sánchez

Finally Casal's dream comes true
Snow falls in Havana

And in the Plaza of the Revolution
there are a multitude of robust firs
covered in garlands

Fulfilling a resolution
of the Central Committee
the small Christmas trees flower

Our monotonous green
becomes what Julián wanted
sprinkled in white

Every dream comes true
Havana falls in snow

CONSIGNAS

Jamás esperas – sólo desesperas
Ni en las casas de empeño
                              he podido encontrarte
Aunque te sé sedienta o vulnerada
no sueño que te entregues
Ultimo triunfo en juego
                              de esta feroz baraja
Dulce sal de la vida

Un delfín es más bello que todas las galaxias
Nada son las estrellas
si no se reflejan en nuestros ojos
Cambio esa sinfonía por una canción
aquella catedral por una casa de tablas
Y dejaré inconcluso este poema
por cambiarle los pañales a mi hijo

Silencio organizado
                              oficio de otro mundo

SLOGANS

You never hope
                    only despair
Not even in pawnshops
                    have I managed to find you
Although I know you to be thirsty or harmed
I don't dream of your surrender
Last trump at stake
                    of this savage shuffle
Sweet salt of life

A dolphin is more beautiful than all the galaxies
The stars are nothing
if they don't reflect in our eyes
I change this symphony for a song
that cathedral for a wooden house
And I'll leave this poem unfinished
to change my son's diapers

Organized silence
                    craft of another world

CONJUROS

Mi madre recoge flores silvestres
entre los árboles de Selva Negra
El pico del tucán
               las plumas de la lapa
el canto del chorlito
                 qué no la embrujen
Y no se quede atrás en el sendero
ni se vaya a perder
                 entre tantos colores
El danto
        la guardatinaja
              el armadillo
qué se aparten de ella
Y acabe de subir esta colina
desde donde hoy la miro
               por primera vez

Esa vela que alumbra
              los ojos de mi madre
La vela desnudísima
con su candela áspera
            y su alma de cera
La vela que no duerme
            deshilando las sombras
La vela que no cesa
de volver luz su miedo
            y quieta se consume
Esa vela que solo
          con tu aliento se aviva
La vela que no logran
a pesar del insomnio
            apagar estos versos

INCANTATIONS

My mother gathers wild flowers
among Black Forest's trees
Tucan's beak
                Macaw's feathers
Dotterel's song
                  may they not bewitch her
And may she not be left behind on the trail
or get lost
             among so many colours
Tapir
     paca
             armadillo
stay far off
And may she finish climbing this hill
where today I see her
                    for the first time

Candle illuminating
                  my mother's eyes
so very naked
with its rough flame
                and wax soul
Sleepless candle
               unravelling shadow
ceaselessly changing
to light its fear
             and quietly is consumed
Candle that only
              with your breath revives
and these verses
in spite of insomnia
              cannot extinguish

AN OREGONIAN POEM

Como ese súbito árbol del norte
cuyo nombre desconoces
                y no sabrás jamás

Arbol de sombra clara
                ya cuajado de nudos
que castigan los vientos sin verano

Arbol para cortar
                de vasto tronco
en donde nadie pudo tatuar un corazón

Arbol que crece solo
                sin raíces evidentes y lejos
del bosque original

Arbol que nada debe
que ha lavado sus culpas
                y es sólo desafío

Como ese árbol eres
                Y en verdad
honra tanta belleza

AN OREGONIAN POEM

As the sudden tree from the north
whose name you do not grasp
                                    and never will

Tree of clear shadow
                        curdled with knots
summerless winds punishing

Tree to be cut
                with vast trunk
where no heart could be carved

Tree rising alone
                        no evident roots and far from
the original forest

Tree owing nothing
has washed its faults
                        and is only defiance

As this tree you are
                        And frankly
such beauty honours us

CONJETURAS SOBRE LA SONRISA DEL PASTOR

para Juan Gil

El pequeño pastor
que cada sábado toca a mi puerta
por Dios
      ¿a quién sonríe?
¿Qué sentido tendrá
la poderosa lumbre de sus dientes?
Esa sonrisa suya
           ¿será la que perdí?

El pequeño pastor
crepuscular
      en el cielo del rostro
¿qué rara estrella luce?
¿La máscara perfecta
         la sonrisa de Dios?
¿Con ella vencerá
la fe inconmovible del ateo?

CONJECTURES ON A PASTOR'S SMILE

for Juan Gil

The little pastor
each Saturday knocks at my door
My God
            who is he smiling at?
Could his teeth's powerful brilliance
have meaning?
                        Could his be the smile I lost?

Twilight's little pastor
                                    in the heavens of his face
what strange star shines?
The perfect mask
                    the smile of God?
With it could he defeat
an atheist's unshakeable faith?

CONFIRMACIONES

para José Pérez Olivares

El menor de mis hijos
                que aún no sabe su nombre
ni caminar derecho
a medianoche
                en la más alta fiebre
                                canta

Es doble este camino
                La razón y la fe
Tengo fe en la razón
                – en la razón impura
Comprendo las razones de la fe
– la fe de los herejes
Entre el hecho y la duda cruzan ambos caminos
Y al partir regresamos

Danza mi rosa ebria
                desprevenida
sin vergüenza del sol
La olvido en el sendero
                que comienza en tus manos
y sin más vueltas me lleva hasta mí

Las preguntas son tigres
                que acechan junto al río
Las respuestas
                ciervos inalcanzables
Mi mucha sed te ahogue
Y náufrago en el polvo
                espera cualquier cosa
menos resignación

CONFIRMATIONS

for José Pérez Olivares

My youngest son
                        who still does not know
his name or how to walk
at midnight
                with highest fever
                                sings

This path is two-way
                        Reason and faith
I have faith in reason –
                        impure reason
I understand the reasons for faith –
heretics' faith
Between fact and doubt both ways cross
And upon leaving we return

Dance my drunken rose
                        unaware
shamelessly of the sun
I forget her on the trail
                        that begins at your hands
and with no more twists leads to me

Questions are tigers
                        crouched by the river
Answers
                unreachable deer
May my great thirst drown you
And though shipwrecked on dust
expect anything
                but resignation

TAROT

para Juan Epple

A la izquierda el amor
                    su flecha única
que atraviesa el vórtice del verano
El tiempo y sus mitades
                    La mujer amarilla
y la mujer azul vuelta de espaldas

La fuerza a la derecha
                    como siempre
La que abre las fauces del león
y lo congela todo con su risa
pero no se echaría
                    la medialuna al hombro

Y más al fondo el sol
                    inevitable
derramando su miel
                    sobre la ambigua torre
La torre que será
                    abolida por el rayo

Al centro la templanza
mezcla desconsolada
                    el agua con el vino
Nadie la ve
          no obstante
su delantal está sucio de estrellas

TAROT

for Juan Epple

On the left love
　　　　　　　its only arrow
crossing summer's vortex
Time and its halves
　　　　　　　　The yellow woman
and the blue woman back turned

Strength on the right
　　　　　　　as always
She who opens the lion's jaws
and freezes everything with her laugh
but would never place
a half moon on her shoulder

And there in the background inevitably
　　　　　　　　　　　　the sun
spilling its honey
　　　　　　　on the ambiguous tower
Tower that will be
　　　　　　　abolished by a ray

In the middle temperance
is mixing inconsolably
　　　　　　　　water with wine
No one sees her
　　　　　yet
her apron is dirty with stars

A BRAVE SUMMER WITH KATE

Te has quitado la máscara
arquera del verano
molesta ya de tanta primavera
Y tu belleza asusta
                    traspasa el corazón
del que sólo cazaba la belleza

Contra siete razones
                    bien armadas y astutas
esgrimo mi sola razón de amor
Y es increíble el daño
que hago con la frágil
                    herrumbrosa espada
que gané a la locura
Retroceden las siete enceguecidas
montan en sus corceles
y me dejan envuelto en este polen
para ninguna flor

Te he visto antes
                    rostro de otros rostros
Yo también perseguía una forma
bajo las armaduras
La forma de tus ojos
que esta noche encandilan mi destino
La forma de tu forma
                    que nadie ha visto antes

De esta tarde de junio
que hasta la propia luz debe mirar
con los ojos cerrados
                    se podría decir
que es la tarde más temprana del mundo
Pero esta tarde es nada
puro infierno de polen
y como esta tarde no tiene tus ojos
simplemente amanece

A BRAVE SUMMER WITH KATE

You have removed your mask
summertime archer
tired of so much spring
And your beauty startles
                              transfixes the heart
of one who only hunted beauty

Against seven reasons
                         well-armed and astute
I wield my only reason of love
And it is incredible the damage
I do with the fragile
                         rusty sword
I won from madness
The seven retreat blinded
mount their steeds
leaving me shrouded in this pollen
for no flower

I have seen you once before
                              face crafted of others
I also pursued a form
beneath the armour
The shape of your eyes
this night kindling my destiny
The structure of your form
                         never seen

Of this June evening
in which light itself must watch
with eyes closed
                    one might say
it is the latest morning in the world
But evening is naught
                         pure pollen hell
and since it does not have your eyes
evening simply dawns

Sin tus ojos
        nadie puede mirar

Te bebo en la cerveza del verano
que mana en esta tregua
                de un trago seco y hondo
Esa cebada negra
que me va llenando de sobriedad
Esa líquida escala que me deja
vísperas del combate
                acceder a tu luz

Yo también soy arquero del verano
puedo flechar la noche
y entregártela
                aún palpitante
sangrando claridad de esta manera
Puedo acertar el día
en su torpe corazón de manzana
y dejarlo tendido
como el amante que espera la ausencia

He puesto estas palabras en mi escudo
por no tachar tu cuerpo
Ya no es mi corazón
                es la flecha que sangra
Tu cuerpo es mi discurso desarmado
la página que escribe

Without your eyes
                    no one may gaze

I taste you in summertime's beer
flowing in this truce
                        of a dry deep drink
Black barley
            fills me with lucidness
Fluid ladder lets me
on the eve of combat
                    gain your light

I am also summertime's archer
I can wound the night with my arrow
and surrender it to you
                        still pounding
bleeding clarity in this way
I can strike daytime
in its clumsy heart of apple
and leave it lying
as a lover awaits absence

I have placed these words on my shield
so to not cross out your body
Now it is not my heart
                        but the arrow bleeding
Your body is my discourse unarmed
the page that writes us

LA SOMBRA DE GÜIRALDES

Güiraldes
        en París
                conversa con el pasto
y cada hoja repite su vida
Los malos pasos de las estaciones
los celos con el sol
la nocturna humillación del rocío
el ansia de la nieve

El gaucho
        como muchos
                se aferra a las palabras
pues teme que la tierra se detenga
y salga proyectado hacia el vacío
Y antes que el cuerpo
                ha echado a volar
su espesa alma infinita

Güiraldes
        en París
                esa pampa de oro
con el pasto conversa
¿Qué nos queda del diálogo?
                La sombra
que ni siquiera mancha
esta hoja sin libro

Quién no quiere juntar
su luz con las estrellas

SHADOW OF GÜIRALDES

Güiraldes
      in Paris
           converses with grass
and each leaf repeats his days
Seasons' false moves
jealous of the sun
dew's nocturnal infamy
snow's anxiousness

The gaucho
      like many
           seizes words
since he fears the planet could stop
launching all toward emptiness
And before his body
          he throws to flight
a thick infinite soul

Güiraldes
      in Paris
         golden pampa
converses with grass
What remains of the dialogue?
          The shadow
not even staining
      this bookless leaf

Who wouldn't hope to join
their light with the stars?

SECRETO PROFESIONAL

El árbol que con desesperación
                              hace gestos al cielo
La mañana que voltea su rostro
salpicado con leche de crepúsculo
El río que de súbito
                    ha perdido la voz
entre la algarabía de las piedras
La sombra del ahorcado
                        su aliento de ceniza
Todo esto tiene
              viajero
                      algo que decirte

Suma
        esa canción descascarada
que ha gritado el olvido
Ese cerro que otra vez se despide
con su pañuelo limpio
donde se puso el sol por cobardía
Esa noche sin pétalos ni fiebre
a pesar del invierno
                      que hoy también claudica
Todo te dice que
              a la muerte
                          no la conocerás

TRADE SECRET

The tree desperately
                   gesturing toward the sky
Daybreak turning its face
sprinkled with twilight's milk
The river that suddenly
                   has lost its voice
among stones' chatter
The hanged man's shadow
                   his ashen breath
All this
        traveller
             has something to tell you

Add to it
        a well-worn song
cried out by oblivion
The hill bidding farewell again
with its clean handkerchief
where the sun set out of cowardice
A night without petals or fire
regardless of the winter
                   that today also yields
All this tells you
             traveller
                death you will not know

ELOGIO DEL NEUTRINO

para Jesús Sepúlveda

Te celebro
            porque en el mundo nadie
es más pequeño que tú
                        y sin embargo
atraviesas galaxias nebulosas estrellas
sin reaccionar con nadie

Porque aún siendo luz
puedes moverte
muchísimo más lento que la luz
o descansar inmóvil
                        corrigiendo
la teoría de un universo caliente

Porque gracias a ti
                        el pasado fue sólo
plasma recalentado y no cenizas
La densidad del plasma
era de billones de toneladas
por centímetro cúbico

Porque nadie sabía
                        hasta ahora
que eras el noventisiete por ciento
de todo
quedando sólo un tres a repartir
entre hijos de puta y demases

Porque gracias a ti
                        nadie se aleja
ya de nadie y todo tiende a unirse
Y no importa que sea
en una llama dura
                        en un punto radiante

EULOGY FOR THE NEUTRINO

for Jesús Selpúveda

I celebrate you
                for in the world no one
is smaller
                and still
you cross galaxies nebulas stars
not reacting

For even being light
                you move
much slower than light
or rest unmoving
                correcting
the theory of a warming universe

For thanks to you
                the past was only
reheated plasma and not ashes
Plasma's density reached
billions of tons
                by cubic centimetre

For no one knew
                until now
you were ninety seven percent
of everything
                leaving only three to be divided up
among sons of bitches and the rest

For thanks to you
                now no one is separated
from anyone and everything tends to unite
And it is not important where
in a solid flame
                at a radiant point

Te celebro
            porque eres
la esencia del espasmo
materia de ternura
                    o ese poco de nada
con que mi tía dora sus natillas

Gracias a Dios
                no es infinito el mundo
Como el verso
                está hecho de sílabas
que es posible contar
El mundo cabe en un alejandrino

I celebrate you
                for you are
                                essence of spasm
matter of tenderness
                        or that tiny bit of nothing
my aunt uses to brown her custards

Thank God
                the world is not infinite
Like verse
                it is made up of syllables
that can be counted
The world fits in an alexandrine

BIOGRAPHICAL NOTES

VÍCTOR RODRÍGUEZ NÚÑEZ is one of Cuba's most noteworthy contemporary writers. He has published eleven books of poetry, many of them recipients of literary awards, including the David Prize (Cuba, 1980), the Plural Prize (Mexico, 1983), the EDUCA Prize (Costa Rica, 1995), the Renacimiento Prize (Spain, 2000), the Fray Luis de León Prize (Spain, 2005) and the Leonor Prize (Spain, 2006). His poems have appeared in *The Kenyon Review, Denver Quarterly, Mid-American Review, Chelsea, New York Quarterly, The Literary Review, New England Review, Circumference, Salt Hill,* and many others internationally. He is an Associate Professor of Spanish at Kenyon College.

KATHERINE M. HEDEEN has a doctorate in Hispanic Literatures from The University of Texas at Austin. She is an Assistant Professor of Spanish at Kenyon College. She specializes in Latin American poetry and has researched about and translated numerous contemporary authors from the region.

Six Slovenian Poets (anthology)
ED. BRANE MOZETIČ
Translated by Ana Jelnikar, Kelly Lenox Allan & Stephen Watts

Six Basque Poets (anthology)
ED. MARI JOSE OLAZIREGI
Translated by Amaia Gabantxo

Six Czech Poets (anthology)
ED. ALEXANDRA BÜCHLER
Translated by Alexandra Büchler, Justin Quinn & James Naughton

A Balkan Exchange:
Eight Poets from Bulgaria & Britain (anthology)
ED. W. N. HERBERT